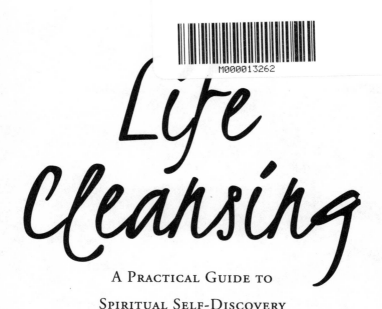

Life Cleansing

A Practical Guide to
Spiritual Self-Discovery

KARIN M. GRAY

— Beaver's Pond Press —
Minneapolis, MN

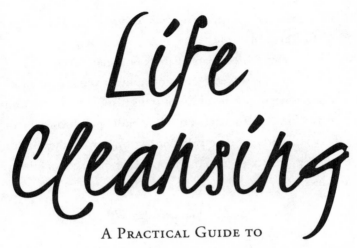

Life Cleansing

A PRACTICAL GUIDE TO
SPIRITUAL SELF-DISCOVERY

KARIN M. GRAY

— BEAVER'S POND PRESS —
Minneapolis, MN

Edited by Kerry Jade Aberman, Angela Wiechmann, and Paige Polinsky

ISBN: 978-1-64343-943-3
Library of Congress Catalog Number: 2019906466
Printed in the United States of America
First Printing: 2019
23 22 21 20 19   5 4 3 2 1

Beaver's Pond Press, Inc.
7108 Ohms Lane
Edina, MN 55439–2129

(952) 829-8818
www.BeaversPondPress.com

To order, visit www.TheLifeCleanser.com.
Reseller discounts available.

This book is for all who have crossed my path in the past, for all who are part of my current path, and for all who are yet to be part of my path.

Thank you, thank you, thank you!

CONTENTS

HOW TO USE THIS BOOK

The only thing that is ultimately real about your journey is the step that you are taking at this moment. That's all there ever is.
—Eckhart Tolle

If you are reading this book, then you have already decided you want to create some type of positive change in your life. Perhaps you seek to understand spiritual experiences and how they can guide you through the change you desire. This book is for anyone—individuals, couples, families—who feels the pull to have it in their hands, regardless of age or gender.

The first thing I want you to understand is that this is *your* journey. There are billions of people in the world, and we are all unique. We each have our own story; we each have our own journey. That is incredible! Others may try to involve or impose themselves in your work by contributing their opinions, but please be strong. Remember that your journey is yours and their journey is theirs, and they are not the same. No other person can control your journey!

This may be your first time using a book as a resource, or it may be your tenth time—that does not matter. The important thing is you see possibility. While having a desired goal or outcome in mind is the starting point, it is actually more important to focus on the process and not get fixated on the end point. What you think needs to be changed may not be what the Universe has in mind for you; it may be something you never even thought of or imagined. You need to trust yourself and the Universe, do the work, and learn as you go. In doing so, you just may be surprised by what amazing gifts come your way.

Using *Life Cleansing*

When you think about *Life Cleansing,* picture a mirror that has been in storage for years and never wiped clean—or perhaps years of layers of polish on a piece of furniture. *Life Cleansing* is the process of removing that buildup, layer by layer, to return the object back to its original beauty and purpose.

Now, replace *object* with *you. Life Cleansing* is about starting from where you are, wiping away all the things that no longer serve you or add value, physically or emotionally, to your life so you can accomplish what may be hiding within. You must work through the layers to get to what is underneath; only then can you see what really needs to be done to bring about the change you need.

Life Cleansing also involves using what the Universe provides and reveals to you. This book explains some of the ways the Universe came through to help me understand where my barriers existed. It also explains how homework made me dig deep and how I used my discoveries to validate my true self, strengthen my resolve, heal my emotional wounds, and take action in my life.

You can apply *Life Cleansing* to anything, small or large, whether it is something you want to obtain or achieve or something you want to purge or organize. There will be times when you feel really vulnerable, challenged, and maybe even exhausted, but that is good. It means you are opening yourself to what you need to receive.

The energizing format of this book allows you to start your path of discovery by opening to any section. Whichever page you open to, that is where your soul wants you to begin… and I will be there to guide you. You get to choose when or how often you explore these pages. Every day of your life is different from the day before—thoughts, feelings, experiences—trust that you will open to what you need. You may even start asking yourself why the Universe led you to a particular page or section. That is part of the excitement and mystique of self-discovery.

Chapter Structure

To help this book feel comfortable, each chapter has a similar format of providing information, experiences, discovery exercises, questions, and *Life Cleansing* applications. As everything in this book is for the purposes of learning, discovery, and teaching, I sometimes refer to the exercises as *homework*. As you work through them, you will find yourself naturally changing how you think and approach situations and experiences as they happen; I sometimes refer to this as *processing*. You will begin to trust your intuition and let it guide you.

Cleansing Tools

While the most important tool is an open mind, here are a few others to consider:

- **Journal:** Selecting your journal is an interesting discovery exercise in itself. Why did you choose the one you did? Did you buy just one or many of the same? How did the purchase make you feel?

- **Writing Instrument:** This can be a similar experience to selecting your journal. Did you select a pen or a marker? What color ink? Did you buy one or many?

- **Space:** While a calm, quiet location is recommended, pick the place that is right for you. Sometimes quiet feels right; other times, you may prefer being in an active environment, such as a café, a library, or some other public place. Meditation or other calming music or sounds may also be something you enjoy. I encourage you to try different environments—go back to the space(s) where you felt the most receptive energy.

- **Openness:** Lastly, allow yourself to be vulnerable. Be *honest* with yourself, embrace compassion for yourself and others, and be grateful.

Please do not think all the experiences in this book need to happen for you or that you must complete the process quickly...*Life Cleansing* is a continuous cycle. This type of work takes a lot of vulnerability, courage, patience, and trust, and I have had much time to experience, absorb, and process the elements of my self-discovery. There is a lot of information shared in this book, so please take your time. It can seem overwhelming at times, but it is so worth it. So are you.

What would life be if we had no courage to attempt anything?
—Vincent van Gogh

Use this book—jot down notes in the margins, highlight or mark parts that resonate with your life, and note when you feel a hit of energy on a topic. My hope for you is that, when you finish the last page (or any page), you will feel strong, healthy, validated, passionate, and energized. You are capable, and you are worthy of all that you wish for.

Please be sure to read the following section, "Message from the Author," as it provides an important look into my own *Life Cleansing* experience as well as why and how this book came to be.

MESSAGE FROM THE AUTHOR

Life is an incredible gift and involves constant reflection, discovery, validation, and change. Every moment, every day, is a continuous cycle of life, death, and rebirth.

—Karin M. Gray

On a last-moment trip a few years ago, I had an unplanned opportunity to meet a person who helped me understand and validate my psychic and intuitive abilities. Through a lot of intense homework, she also helped me to understand my core issue and sabotaging habits as well as to identify, understand, and own my higher purpose.

That purpose is to guide you, to teach you what I have learned and experienced, and to do so in a way that allows you to remain grounded in the physical third dimension while also discovering and accessing the spiritual dimension. I believe a person can be more successful in creating change if all possibilities are explored and utilized.

Since I was a small child, I have experienced things I could not explain and that were definitely coming through a spiritual or other-dimensional place. You will read about many of them in the pages that follow. These experiences intensified through my adult years to the point where I had to explore my curiosity. I had to understand what these visions and experiences meant. I also knew that my career direction was changing, that I was being led down a path I had never imagined or expected. Once I gained greater insight into my higher purpose, it became clear that the Universe was moving me forward to teach me what I would need and how to get there.

It is now my honored responsibility to put myself and my purpose out into the world. I am grateful that you are part of this gift I have been given and that we are on this journey together. It is exciting to know that every day there is something new to feel, observe, discover, and learn.

If you are interested, at any point, in learning more about *Life Cleansing* and how we may work and discover together, please visit my website at **www.thelifecleanser.com**.

I now release my words to you.

INTRODUCTION

What is cleansing?

Cleanse: to rid of impurities by or as if by washing; to engage in or undergo a cleanse to remove toxins from the body. Related words: amend, improve, refine, heal, regenerate, restore, uplift, absolve, clear, decontaminate, disinfect, straighten (up), unclutter.[1]

Before my own *Life Cleansing* . . .

- **I was going through the motions, very successfully, for years.** Others thought I had it all together; my life seemed perfect, and I was very good at appearing happy. What people did not know was that I was functioning like a robot, but with a smile. I got out of bed early in the morning, got through my workday,

---

1. *Merriam-Webster's Collegiate Dictionary*, 11th ed. (Springfield, MA: Merriam-Webster, 2003). Also available at www.merriam-webster.com.

went home, got through my evening, and went to bed . . . to start all over again the next day.

- *I was completely burned out in my profession.* I was the person who strove to be the best at anything I did, especially in work. I gave everything I had to every employer, and that made me very successful in my profession. I received promotions, pay raises, and other perks, along with increased responsibility. I gave so much to my work that I often did not have anything left for anyone else. After thirty years of this, I was completely fried. It got to the point that it was all I could do to get myself out of bed in the morning.

- *I was emotionally drained, depressed, devoid of feeling, and shut down.* I was a shell of my former self. The only feelings I could think of were sadness, loneliness, and fear; I could not think beyond those feelings. I did not want to burden others with these feelings. When I did try to talk to some people, they said what I was going through was normal and everything would be fine. They would then change the subject to something they wanted to talk about. So, I closed myself off even more. I became dead inside.

- *I was in danger of losing "me" forever.* I was so sad to think I would have to live this way indefinitely. I was so afraid of never feeling happy or excited or

passionate about anything again—I was too young to
live such a sad and lonely existence.

Now, this is where I need to tell you that this book is not
about doom and gloom. It is about hope, discovery, possibilities, and action.

Once I realized I had reached my lowest point, I knew
I had to check in with myself. I needed to take back control
of my thoughts, my emotions, my actions, and my behaviors. I did not know how; I just knew I had to do something,
and medication was not going to be the answer for me. So,
I took action inspired by a period in my late twenties, back
when I completed my first intentional and intense self-reflection process. Once again, I put my trust in the Universe, and
my world started to change more than I could have possibly
imagined. Before I knew it, the Universe placed events and
people in my path that I needed, and I am so grateful.

So, what happened?

- *Just when I was considering leaving, my job of
  almost twenty years was eliminated as part of a
  corporate restructure.* My first thought was to take
  my severance pay and run. My second thought was
  to consider another opportunity in the company
  and continue earning a good income with benefits. The more I considered staying, the worse it felt.
  Ultimately, I chose to leave the company and my

thirty-year career with no regrets. My job loss was the Universe giving me a big push. Thank you.

- *Just a couple of weeks after leaving the company, one of my sisters called me. She asked if I would be interested in going with her, her youngest son, and our mom to visit an aunt and cousin in Montana.* As I was no longer working, I said I would. We left just a couple of weeks after that initial phone call. Aside from spending time in the beautiful mountains of Montana, I also had the unexpected and life-changing opportunity to meet Carolyn, a medical intuitive (herein referred to as my mentor). Finally, I had someone I could talk to about a number of experiences I have had over my life, such as having recurring and intensely realistic dreams, finding pennies, feeling energy in places, having insights into people upon meeting them, and being visited by many spirits. I knew she was the reason the Universe led me to Montana. Over the time I worked with her, I had a number of emotional meltdowns, but they were all good. Each meltdown meant that I was finally opening myself up to rebuild and heal. I felt hopeful. Thank you.

- *Next came an emotionally difficult period of evaluating the relationships in my life.* During such important evaluations, you need to look at each person in your life and understand their impact—how they make you feel and what happens to your energy when you are around them. This includes relationships with family members, significant others, friends, coworkers, and other acquaintances. You must decide if their energy is positively or negatively impacting you.

In my personal situation, this led to acknowledging I needed to leave my marriage and ultimately move to a new area. It was the most difficult thing I have ever had to do, but it was also very necessary. Staying would have hurt many people over time, which was the last thing I ever wanted to do. It took a tremendous amount of emotional work, strength, and time spent understanding why I needed to leave and what I truly wanted my life to look like—what I needed it to be. The Universe helped me by opening me up spiritually, teaching me to connect energetically, and revealing to me what I needed and when I needed it. Thank you.

- *While I had started writing a book about twelve years prior to the book you are now reading, the original book was related to my profession. As I knew my career path was changing, it became clear that the focus of my book also needed to change.* Following my divorce and settling into my new home, there was a night when a dream provided me with a very strong vision of what my book was meant to be . . . and you are now reading it. It was during my discovery journey that I began to further define my higher purpose: to be a teacher and to help people on their journeys. Part of my higher purpose was to write this book—the content needed to come from my life, what I knew, and what I had experienced.

Writing a book is still one of the scariest things I have done—it is the ultimate vulnerability, sharing your thoughts and experiences for the world to read and knowing they will form an impression (good, bad, or indifferent) beyond your control. I had to stay focused, trust the process, and complete what I was meant to do. The Universe put the right people on my path to help make my book and my business a reality. Thank you.

- *Traveling is one of my passions. It was also during my discovery journey that I chose to book myself an amazing monthlong trip to England, Wales, Ireland, Northern Ireland, and Scotland.* This trip was a vision quest—an energy connection of past lives (there will be more on this later in the book), an experience to explore through a spiritual perspective, and an opportunity to just have an adventure. I was blessed to travel with forty-four other people, and every one of us was meant to be there. The experience was life-changing for me. The Universe definitely did its work to put those people and places in my path. Thank you.

- ***While my journey continues among many paths, I am now living my purpose, honoring my self-integrity, owning my spiritual power, and living in passion, compassion, and gratitude.*** Thank you, thank you, thank you!

We all have our own stories and reasons for seeking. Whether you feel you are stuck in life, you are seeking something and not finding it, you want to get organized, or you are just incredibly curious . . . this book is for you. It is a safe space for you to explore your deeper self. I will be with you as you travel its pages and work through your discovery exercises.

I want it to feel like we are sitting down together and having a conversation. So, get your pen and journal, find your special place, get comfy, and let us begin.

Part 1

LAYERS: FINDING WHAT IS BELOW THE SURFACE

CLARIFYING EXPECTATIONS

Though no one can go back and make a brand-new start, anyone can start from now and make a brand-new ending.
—*Carl Bard*

Do you ever catch yourself doing something you do not like and ask, *Why am I doing this?* For instance, maybe you are accepting a leadership position even though you prefer more hands-on work. Maybe you are acting like one person when around one group of people and then being another person around a different group of people. Or maybe you find yourself doing activities you do not enjoy because you do not want to hurt anyone's feelings by declining. In these and similar scenarios, chances are you have allowed another person's expectations to become your own. Unfortunately, if you do not recognize this, you may one day wake up wondering what happened.

⫸⫸⫸ DISCOVERY EXERCISE ⫷⫷⫷

Are you living based on the expectations of others? Write down your responses to the following questions.

- What are you doing in your life currently that you do not feel connected to?

- Do you enjoy your current employment/ profession?

- Do you have relationships that drain your energy/spirit/self?

- Do you often participate in activities even though you really do not want to?

- Do you talk yourself into thinking something is right for you because others told you to do it or said you would be good at it?

- Do you agree to things because you do not want to hurt other people's feelings?

- Do you hold back from expressing your thoughts or opinions out of fear of offending someone else or thinking their thoughts are better than yours?

- Do you talk yourself out of doing things before you even begin?

- Have you ever gotten burned out doing something you thought you enjoyed or were good at?

- Do you hold back sharing things about your true self out of fear of judgment from others?

Were you surprised by your responses? How did this exercise make you feel?

Until I went through my own *Life Cleansing,* I realized I had lived most of my life based on the wants, needs, and expectations of others—my family, friends, and colleagues. While I thought I was in control and doing what I wanted, I came to understand that my expectations were really those of others that I had taken on as my own. People complimented my abilities and encouraged me to pursue this or that. I took on more and more, and I became more and more unhappy along the way.

It took extreme burnout and depression for me to realize I was not being true to myself. I was not honoring myself; I was not listening to myself, and I was not expressing myself. It was a sad, disappointing realization. I have always been a strong woman who tries to make her own choices, but I had created an exterior based on what other people wanted and expected of me.

I was many months into my self-discovery and home-work before I shared anything about it. It just felt really important for me to *protect* myself in that first year until I felt stronger. You, too, get to decide if, what, or how much you will share with others.

It is possible that when you start rediscovering yourself and experiencing personal transformation, people will notice. They will ask you about what has changed. Some will challenge the concepts in this book—and you along with them—and I want you to be prepared. I experienced it myself: that "are you crazy?" kind of look.

When this happens, be thoughtful. Acknowledge how they feel, and let them know it is OK for them to question or disbelieve your discovery process. However, also ask them to respect you and your decisions. Explain that you are doing what is right for *you* and will not change who you are, just as they should not change for you.

You cannot change others, but you can change yourself. You can change how you react to everyone and everything around you. That is a great and powerful ability.

TIME TO CLEAN YOUR SELF-HOUSE

The greatest waste in the world is the difference between what we are and what we could become.

—*Ben Herbster*

Are you seeking or craving *something* that you cannot quite identify? Do you feel antsy, edgy, discontented, or in a rut?

If yes, you are likely someone who will try this and that in hope of figuring it out. When those efforts do not work, you will again try this or try that, only for those attempts to fail too. If this sounds like you, you are what I call a *searcher*. You are rarely happy in your situation and always looking for something new to bring you fulfillment (e.g., a different job, a promotion, a new boss, a new relationship, etc.). But it only leads to frustration and misguided choices.

What people often miss is that these feelings of discontent are really a message. The Universe is telling you it is time for change; you are veering off your path and need to plot a new direction.

When I would get this way at work, I knew it was time to do some decluttering and reorganizing to help clear my space and my mind so I could focus on the problem. Then I would work on my perspective and attitude, make a game plan, and get back to work. This would help for a while—sometimes weeks and sometimes months. But when that antsy feeling returned, I knew the problem was more than just being overwhelmed with the work; it was the job itself.

People experience frustration in all areas of life. As the world seems to spin increasingly out of control, many feel like their own control is slipping away. Add the various forms of media (news and social) into that spiral, along with a lot of blaming and toxic banter, and it is no wonder we are always searching for *something* to help us feel calm and in control.

⟫⟫ DISCOVERY EXERCISE ⟪⟪

Consider the following list of things you can do to help bring you back to yourself and into a feeling of ownership for your life.

● Stop and pay attention to your true feelings.

- Pay attention to the environment around you; the Universe is providing you with helpful messages, but you are not seeing them. These messages may be coming to you in the form of signs, symbols, dreams, visions, visits, energies, or intuitions.

- Concentrate less on controlling your environment and more on connecting your own energy to the universal connection we all share. Bring that energy inward; break the habits and patterns causing friction and holding you back.

- Focus on changing what you can, such as your thoughts, actions, reactions, and behaviors.

- Spend time in nature. Be present in the moment and use your senses (sight, smell, hearing, touch, taste, and energy) to feel whatever comes through. This is key to *Life Cleansing*.

Recognize when something is ending and needs to change, work to understand what that something is, and figure out what then needs to be created. This is the perfect time for *Life Cleansing*. Trust your intuition; do not ignore it. Be open and honest, and do not worry about any limitations that try to seep into your thoughts. Reflect on the *what* and the *why* before focusing on the *how*.

⇒⇒⇒ DISCOVERY EXERCISE ⇐⇐⇐

What is on your mind?

1. List every area in your life where you want to see change (e.g., work, family, relationships, volunteerism, education, finances, religion or spirituality, fun).

2. Write down the specific things in those areas that you want to change. It does not matter how small or large they are. Do not let yourself become overwhelmed with this part—just get it all out. There are no right or wrong answers.

3. Write down how each of those answers makes you feel. Naming your feelings will help determine where you are placing the most energy and where you need to begin focusing your work.

⇒⇒⇒ DISCOVERY EXERCISE ⇐⇐⇐

Look at your list from the exercise above. With it in mind, spend some quality time on the following.

1. What do you want your life or a particular situation

to be/look like?

2. Take time to focus on what that really looks like—picture it, internalize it.

3. Write down how that vision makes you feel.

As you progress, this is an especially good exercise to come back to. It will serve as a point of calibration and reflection.

⋙ DISCOVERY EXERCISE ⋘

Get to know yourself from a different perspective. While writing in a restaurant, it hit me that life is like a menu . . . a menu of you. Your menu includes appetizers, main courses, side dishes, condiments, and desserts.

Write down your responses to the following:

● What do you need to get started, to whet your appetite?

● What are you hungry for?

● What would complement the main course?

● What do you need to make it taste a little better?

● What is for dessert (i.e., your reward)?

Now, think gourmet:

- **Recipe:** What are your core ingredients? What traits, characteristics, and qualities are you made of? What do you want to be made of?

- **Toppings:** What are those little extras that make you better? Perhaps your smile, your hairstyle, your handshake, your approachability. . . .

- **Specialties:** What makes you unique? What special talents do you have?

The previous exercises got you started. Now, it is time to think about your wishes and how to bring them into reality.

Your first thought might be that wishes are selfish. Wishes are really just a statement of what you want in your life. There is nothing wrong with wishes; they give you hope and things to strive for. Wishes can also represent your aspirations and your passions; you do not have to limit them to your lists from above. When you wish, when you imagine, when you are curious, your soul is speaking to you. With that, please be free with your wishes.

Caution: Make sure the wishes reflect what you want and not what someone else wants for you. They can make their own wishes!

⫸⫸⫸ DISCOVERY EXERCISE ⫷⫷⫷

Set aside some time to create your wish board. You may want to work on it over several days. Release all restrictions your mind wants to put in place and just let your heart lead you.

1. List *everything* you wish for. Do not worry about how the wishes will happen; just focus on stating them. *Note: It is up to you if you want this to be your wish board for the year, a few years, ten years, or even more.*

2. Look at your list and note if there are any similar items or those that belong on a general to-do list— then remove them. Next, make sure the remaining wishes truly represent your chosen time period. Some things may take longer than you want, but you should still include them on the board. Remember, what you want may not be what the Universe has planned for you.

3. Using your list, search websites, magazines, or other media to find images that best represent your wishes. Some may be tangible (earning a certain income, achieving a health goal, traveling places, etc.), and some may be intangible (a value

by which you want to live your life, such as compassion or philanthropy).

4. Cut your favorite images out (if they are digital, arrange them in an electronic document and print it) and adhere them to a board. If you like, draw frames around them or pair them with short, motivating captions. *Note: You can display your wish board in any form—on paper, on poster or foam board, or even as an electronic document for your computer screen saver. Be creative!*

5. Display the finished wish board where you can see it often. It is up to you if you want to display it where others can see.

6. Internalize your wishes so you feel like they are all truly possible . . . after all, they are! I taped my first wish boards to a large whiteboard along with the following written mantra: *"Everything I wish for is within me because I am healthy, strong, worthy, capable, and grateful . . . in body, mind, and spirit."* I would look at my board and repeat this mantra daily, sometimes multiple times a day. (I still do with the electronic wish board I create each year). This is a very empowering exercise.

Once you make your wishes, do not forget to check in with your attitude. You may say that nothing good ever happens to you or that you are not lucky. But if that is the vibe you are putting out there, then that is what you are drawing into your life. In a sense, you are wishing for the negative to occur.

Example: Instead of saying you no longer want to be in debt, say that you wish to have $10,000 in your savings account by a specific date—take the focus off debt and place it on money in the bank.

Example: Instead of saying you do not want to be overweight, say that you will commit to working out four times a week—take the focus off being overweight and place it on leading a healthy lifestyle.

Shift your mind-set to focus on what you *do* want, not what you *do not* want. In other words, focus on positivity and gratitude. Visualize the best outcome—that is what you want to put out to the Universe. Once you do that, pay attention! The strength and authenticity of your wishes come from within.

If you just read through the wish board exercise and are having trouble making your wishes or are hesitant to ask for what you want, doing an imagination exercise may help. Some may call this *daydreaming*. I think children are the best at it; give a child a cardboard box and see what happens.

Imagine—to form a mental image of (something not present); to form a notion of without sufficient basis; to think of or create (something that is not real) in your mind (*Merriam-Webster*).

⇒⇒⇒ **DISCOVERY EXERCISE** ⇐⇐⇐

It is time to imagine. Do this exercise as often as you want. After all, it does not cost anything to imagine.

1. Pick a time when it feels right to sit in a distraction-free space by yourself. Close your eyes, breathe, and clear your mind for a couple of minutes.

2. Keeping your eyes closed, ask your soul to wander.

3. Where does it go first? Stay with it and see it through to the final scene.

4. Open your eyes and write your experience down.

5. How did you feel about the things you saw?

At this time, you may be wondering *how* to make your wishes happen. You cannot just sit back and wait for them to become reality; you have to do your part. When you look at your wish board, think about steps you can take to help the process. Your actions can be large or small; it does not matter so long as you are doing *something*. Sometimes you just need to complete that first action item and then the Universe will help you with the rest. So, pay attention not only to what is revealed to you but also to your feelings and intuition. Listen to your gut.

Be flexible and willing to go with the flow . . . wishes often do not respond well to rigidity.

Wishes give you hope and keep you moving forward. Keep them alive in your heart and in front of you; meditate on them and release them to the Universe.

Also consider how you will receive what comes to you. Will you be patient with the understanding that what you wish for will come to you when the time is right (and only if the wish will serve your higher purpose), or will you be impatient and allow your personal frustration to blind you?

For a moment, fast-forward to reflect on the year prior. My favorite time to do this is in the last week of December, when I create my wish board for the new year. This reflection always energizes me and serves as great validation.

⋙ DISCOVERY EXERCISE ⋘

Focus on all that you have and all the things you have accomplished.

1. Set up your environment. Choose a quiet place and have your pen and journal ready. Perhaps prepare some tea or another calming beverage, light a candle or two, and play some relaxing music in the background. Or, if you prefer, surround yourself

with active energy and turn up the volume of your favorite music. Do whatever works for you.

2. Allow yourself dedicated time to meditate (refer to the chapter "Creating Intention with Meditation").

3. Write down all that you accomplished over the year. (I keep a lot of notes on my electronic calendar, which is very helpful in this process.) These accomplishments can relate to any area of your life. Be sure to include everything you can think of, not just the items on your wish board. You may be surprised at all the things you did that were actually somehow related to a wish but maybe were not the completion of the full wish itself.

4. Take a moment to give yourself credit for your accomplishments, no matter how large or small, and be grateful.

5. If you have interest in stars and numbers, this is a time to review what was predicted for your birth date in the prior year. It is also an opportunity to read the prediction for your birth date in the coming year. After reading this, put it away until your reflection process the following year.

6. In addition to creating a wish board, I also make penny wishes in a little fountain. This step is completely up to you. Here is what I do: I put my new wish board in front of me and, one at a time, I state a wish and drop a penny in my fountain. *Note: You may want to add a new wish or two throughout the year . . . Go for it! Your wishes are yours!*

7. Close with dedicated meditation. Release your wishes to the Universe. Let the new year begin!

Do you ever wish you could just snap your fingers and all that you desire would just appear? Do you wish you had a crystal ball to reveal all of life's answers? You may especially feel this way when the road gets tough and you are tired of doing all the work *Life Cleansing* involves. As doubt, fear, and insecurity work their way back in, you may start to question everything all over again.

When this happens, remind yourself of what you are trying to accomplish and push forward. Let go of the control you are gripping so tightly. It is time to trust the Universe; pay attention to what is being shown to you, and let things happen as they are meant to. You have to do the work to earn the reward. Keep your eyes on your wish board!

Focusing on your wishes allows you to keep out the things that do not serve you or your higher purpose. It allows you to curb the clutter and clean out what does not belong, physically and emotionally. When you fill your life with the things that add value, a natural *Life Cleansing* process occurs. However, you need to do your homework. There are action items along the way, and there will certainly be more to do after you read this book. Practice patience, embrace the journey, and also have some fun!

This is where you may expect to hear me say, "May your dreams come true." Well, as I thought about that, I really do not want your "dreams" to come true.

Most of my dreams are made of some pretty crazy stuff because my subconscious is trying to give me messages through dreams that are to guide, lead, and validate. Many dreams do not make much sense—at least not until they are interpreted. Through many layers, dreams show you how to make your wishes happen . . . if you are willing to do the work.

So, I say to you, "May your *wishes* come true."

THE REFLECTION IN YOUR MIRROR

The only person you are destined to become is the person you decide to be.

—*Ralph Waldo Emerson*

A big part of the *Life Cleansing* process is to do homework on yourself. It is easy to get so wrapped up in your life that you do not take the time to check in with yourself. Sometimes, your life may feel like it is owned and manipulated by others, and that is why self-reflection is so critical.

I suspect most of you will want to skip the first exercise in this chapter, but please do not do that. It is time to look in the mirror. (Yes, you read that correctly.)

Have you ever sleepily walked into the bathroom in the morning, looked at yourself in the mirror, and thought, *Who is that?* or *Is that really what I look like?* At this time, you may realize your physical self is showing signs something may not be going too well with your inner or emotional self. That can be scary. Use this next exercise to really look at yourself; be open to whatever you see.

➤➤➤ DISCOVERY EXERCISE ◄◄◄

Look in the mirror and see what is reflected. A full-length mirror is preferable, but a large mirror will do.

1. Stand in front of the mirror and take a look at your whole body.

2. Spend time looking at just your face.

3. Really look into your eyes (your window inward).

Now, I want you to write down your answers to the following questions. It is critical that you are honest, as it does not do any good to lie to yourself. If you go to a sad or unhappy place during this exercise, please know that this is just one step in discovery . . . positive action will follow.

1. What were your first thoughts? What did you say to yourself?

2. What did you see?

3. How did you feel? Write down what you were feeling in that moment, not how you want to feel in the future (to trick yourself into thinking you are feeling fine about something when you are really not).

The process of change rarely starts with feeling good about the situation you are trying to change. I want you to do this exercise about every three to six months. As you cleanse things away, you will start to see yourself differently. I was shocked when I did this exercise for the first time and did my check-in a few months later; I almost cried at the positive difference—not so much in my physical body yet but in my face and especially in my eyes. This exercise is always a good way to gauge your physical and emotional status. Do you look tired and sad or refreshed and energized?

If you chose not to do the mirror exercise, why did you decide not to do it? Be brutally honest. Your answer to this question may be more revealing than if you had done the exercise itself.

Next, I want you to get to know yourself in another way. This exercise is easier and more fun, but I still want you to take it seriously.

⫸ DISCOVERY EXERCISE ⫷

What are your favorite things? For each one, write down *why* it is your favorite and also how each one makes you *feel.*

1. What is your favorite movie?

2. What is your favorite song?

3. What is your favorite book?

4. What is your favorite color?

5. What is your favorite car?

6. What is your favorite meal?

7. What is your favorite beverage?

8. What is your favorite snack?

9. What is your favorite food seasoning?

10. What is your favorite hobby?

11. What is your favorite animal?

12. What is your favorite place?

13. What is your favorite time of year?

14. What is your favorite ice cream flavor?

15. What is your favorite part of your body?

16. What is your favorite place in your home?

17. What is your favorite band/musician?

18. What is your favorite instrument?

19. What is your favorite game?

20. What is your favorite sport?

21. What is your favorite flower?

22. What is your favorite tree?

23. What is your favorite piece of jewelry?

24. What is your favorite piece of furniture?

25. What is your favorite holiday?

26. What is your favorite television show?

27. What is your favorite fruit?

28. What is your favorite vegetable?

29. What is your favorite candy?

30. What is your favorite time of day?

31. What is your favorite type of clothing?

32. What is your favorite vacation destination?

33. What is your favorite style of home?

34. What is your favorite subject of conversation?

35. What is your favorite childhood memory?

36. What is your favorite adulthood memory?

37. Who is your favorite friend?

38. Who is your favorite superhero?

39. Who is your favorite actor?

40. Who is your favorite cartoon character?

You may also do this exercise by answering with your least favorite things, as that may provide some valuable insights as well.

For another perspective, I want you to now think back over your entire life.

⇒⇒⇒ DISCOVERY EXERCISE ⇐⇐⇐

What are you still giving energy to from your past?

1. Close your eyes, focus on your breathing, and clear your mind.

2. Write down a chronology of key moments in your life up until today. Do this in one sitting and do not think about it too long; just start writing.

Now, write down your answers to the following questions:

- Why do these memories still come to mind?

- How do these memories make you feel?

- Do you want to let these memories go? Do you want to release the energetic hold they have on you? If not, why?

Most, if not all, of us have had hard times in our life that were really difficult to get through. It is so important to not let those times control your present. *Please* do not try to compare stories with others to see who had it worse. Playing the one-up game is so damaging and does not serve any purpose but to make you and others spiral into negativity. Keep your focus on discovery and cleansing. It is possible you may not realize which key moments from your past are still impacting you, but they are often the root of limiting habits and patterns. This is not an exercise for pointing fingers and placing blame on others; it is about self-discovery and positive action.

The next exercise is also very helpful in recognizing habits and patterns. For me, it was both incredibly eye-opening and sad; there, on paper, were all the opportunities I let pass me by. However, it also motivated me to start changing my thoughts so that I could ultimately change my actions, which then helped me break those ingrained, limiting habits and patterns.

While doing my homework, I realized all the opportunities I wanted but did not take were missed out of fear. However, fear alone was not an acceptable answer; I had to keep digging to get to what was really going on. I sadly discovered that my fear was rooted in inferiority and insecurity, and I traced these feelings all the way back to childhood. On the surface, these were the last things people would have expected me to feel because I compensated in other ways. It was a critical moment of discovery. I sat in the moment and cried . . . and then I went into action mode. Discovery and growth are always about movement.

⋙ DISCOVERY EXERCISE ⋘

Reflect on what you *could have* done.

- Write down as many things that you can think of that you *could have* done in your life but you chose not to.

- Write down why you did not do them.

- Write down your feelings with each situation.

> • Do you see a particular feeling or pattern? This
> is a very interesting part of the process. This is
> the root (core) of discovery and where change
> starts to happen.

Through this exercise, you will really start to gain insight into your *core issue.* I reference this term throughout the book.

So, what is a core issue? When you embark on a transformational journey, it is because you are being led to solve an issue linked to your soul energy. You are feeling called to do something different with your life, but to move forward, you must first resolve or cleanse your soul so it can mature. While you may have more than one core issue, you will typically be led to work on the most prevalent one with smaller issues being resolved in parallel. Once you identify your core issue through the process of discovery homework, its limiting barriers will begin to fall away; your true self will be revealed and led to live its higher purpose.

My core issue: I dismissed my self-integrity and spiritual power. *This became increasingly clearer to me as I progressed through my homework assignments and really started to see the habits and patterns sabotaging my true self. I surrendered my voice, feelings, ideas, and even my worth to make things easier or more comfortable for others and to avoid conflict. I did not want to damage relationships or appear too strong or opinionated. While others could say whatever they wanted or thought, I almost* *always got shut down, interrupted, or ignored. If I spoke from a different or opposing perspective, I was thought to be bitchy (how dare I not agree with the other person's views!) or judgmental. However, I was expected to accept all that others said with full attention and agreement.*

I often felt disappointed in others because I allowed them their voice and to be who they were but they did not afford me the same opportunity. At the same time, I had to accept my own role in that—I did not speak up and stand my ground. I truly believe that had I not experienced my own Life Cleansing *journey, I would have gone to my grave feeling that I was not valued for my true self, that I did not belong, that I was an outsider, that I was just there physically but not emotionally, that I was not the person I could have been.*

Your core issue will be unique to you. All the discovery exercises in this book are for you. However, I think self-integrity is something we should all strive for and ensure we are honoring. Self-integrity is about self-truth; it is about owning and honoring who you are and what you believe.

I encourage you to create a statement of integrity about yourself and modify it as you move through your journey. After months of intense homework, this is my own statement of self-integrity. It no longer describes who I want to be; it reflects who I am.

I am a strong, independent, free-thinking, intelligent, passion-ate, interesting, adventurous, reflective, and compassionate woman. I own my self-integrity, honor my spiritual power, and find ways to live my purpose and the life I want.

In addition, I wrote a statement describing how those qualities will show up in my life:

My integrity is about living life as my true self by respecting my values and ethics and communicating when they are being compromised by others; using my knowledge, skills, experience, and abilities to help others; continuing to explore and go on new adventures; being compassionate toward others; taking care of myself; and having gratitude for everything.

⫸ **DISCOVERY EXERCISE** ⫷

Create your statement of integrity. *Note: You can come back to this exercise as often as you need to. You can revise it as many times as you need to before feeling it is complete.*

1. Take a minute to just breathe and open yourself to what is inside you, in your heart.

2. Write down words that you feel represent who you truly are, not just on the surface or what others say about you.

3. Form your statement using those words.

4. Read the statement aloud to yourself. How does it make you feel?

5. When you feel your statement of self-integrity is in its final form, say it to yourself over and over again. Internalize it, live it, breathe it!

Now, with your statement in mind, write down how your self-integrity will show up in your life.

Living your truth requires devotion and tirelessness. Do not give your power and integrity to others to manage. It is yours—own it! If you stay true to yourself and your purpose, the Universe will be there with you providing guidance and opportunities.

Be yourself; everyone else is already taken.

—*Oscar Wilde*

Do not wait for others to validate all that is good about you. Validate yourself!

DIGGING THROUGH YOUR FEELINGS

The best way out is always through.

—*Robert Frost*

I have already asked you to work with your feelings in prior exercises, and I will in future chapters as well. Feelings are your gauge. Feelings, good or bad, are what make us human, and, as humans, we have the ability to adjust those feelings.

When I started my transformational journey, the only feelings I could name were *sad, lonely,* and *afraid.* Despite being a strong and independent woman, I used those words to describe just about everything. I was so disconnected from my feelings. I had been hiding from my feelings for so long.

Almost all the homework assignments required me to work through my feelings, which was a real struggle. I even turned to the Internet, searching for lists of feelings because I did not know what words to use. Sometimes my feelings were a combination of things, and I just had to keep digging until I got to the right description. Deciding how you really feel about something can be quite intense, but it takes brutal honesty to be true to yourself.

Maybe you cope with feelings by utilizing compartmentalization—putting your feelings about different things into separate compartments and drawing on them only when needed. This is something I starting doing as a child.

Whenever I felt frightened or uncertain, I would retreat into myself and escape into my own special space; having six other siblings, that was not always easy. My coping mechanism was to focus on my belongings and my space. There, I kept things as neat, compact, and organized as I could. I loved containers of all kinds; I created homes for tiny dolls and animal-shaped erasers using empty checkbook boxes. (To this day, I cannot resist examining containers and boxes—especially antiques because they are so much more interesting—opening drawers or lids and peeking inside.) I controlled my space by making my bed as soon as I got out of it, by organizing my dresser drawers, and by filling notepads with neat, tiny writing. I always had a place for everything. My life was all about compartments—physically and emotionally.

⫸ **DISCOVERY EXERCISE** ⫷

How do feelings show up in your life?

- What coping mechanism do you use when you do not want to feel?

- Do you express your feelings in the moment? If not, why?

- How do you express your feelings?

- Do you express your feelings strongly, occasionally, or never?

- How do you react when others express their feelings?

While I do not expect you to constantly monitor your feelings, it is always helpful to be more aware of them as well as whether or not to express them. Sometimes you may use feelings as excuses when you are afraid to do or try something. When you shut down your feelings, you disengage from your life. No matter what, do not bury your feelings. When you have a strong feeling, just sit in it for a moment and think about it. Then decide if any action needs to be taken or if you just want to allow it to pass.

⋙ DISCOVERY EXERCISE ⋘

Reflect on your emotional triggers over the course of two weeks. Each day, write down when your emotions are triggered. Use the following questions as a guide.

- What was the situation?

- Was there a negative trigger?

- Do you want that trigger to control you going forward?

- If it is a bad feeling, how are you going to change it?

- If it is a good feeling, how are you going to re-create it?

Let any negative feelings or reactions move through you and out of you. Learn from them. Ultimately, we all want to feel good, and we all deserve happiness. *Life Cleansing* clears out the negative so you can focus your energy on the positive.

Are you a person who feels like life is all bad? Do not believe it. Redirect that thinking and instead focus on gratitude and positivity. As long as your physical body is still alive, your soul is still alive and present within you; there is still energy within you to make changes, and there is still hope. When you work to change habits, use positive words. For example, instead of saying "I will try to change" or "I should do" something, insert "I am open to changing" or "I am working on doing" whatever is needed.

I purposely did not put this chapter on feelings earlier in the book because I wanted you to access your feelings on your own in those first exercises to help you understand where you are at on the feelings journey—shut down or open. To give you the help I needed, following are some lists I put together of both positive and negative feelings. These are the words I have used most often. If you need help naming your feelings as you go along, come back to these lists or feel free to search for more.

POSITIVE FEELINGS			
Absorbed	Accepting	Admirable	Affectionate
Amazed	Animated	Attracted	Bold
Brave	Calm	Certain	Challenged
Cheerful	Clever	Comfortable	Confident
Considerate	Content	Courageous	Curious
Daring	Eager	Elated	Encouraged
Energized	Engrossed	Enthusiastic	Excited
Fascinated	Feisty	Fortunate	Free
Frisky	Hopeful	Important	Inquisitive
Inspired	Interested	Intrigued	Joyful
Loving	Optimistic	Passionate	Peaceful
Playful	Provocative	Quiet	Reassured
Rebellious	Receptive	Relaxed	Satisfied
Secure	Sensitive	Serene	Surprised
Sympathetic	Thankful	Thrilled	Understanding
Unique	Warm	Yearning	

NEGATIVE FEELINGS			
Aching	Aggressive	Agonized	Anxious
Ashamed	Bored	Cowardly	Crushed
Deprived	Desperate	Diminished	Disappointed
Discouraged	Disgusted	Disillusioned	Disinterested
Dissatisfied	Distrustful	Dominated	Doubtful
Dull	Embarrassed	Empty	Fatigued
Fearful	Frustrated	Grieving	Guilty
Hateful	Heartbroken	Hesitant	Humiliated
Impulsive	Incapable	Incensed	Indecisive
Inferior	Infuriated	Insecure	Insensitive
Irritated	Isolated	Lifeless	Lonely
Lost	Miserable	Mournful	Offended
Pained	Paralyzed	Pathetic	Pessimistic
Powerless	Preoccupied	Provoked	Rejected
Resentful	Reserved	Restless	Shaky
Shy	Skeptical	Sorrowful	Stressed
Sulky	Suspicious	Tense	Terrified
Threatened	Timid	Tormented	Uncertain
Uneasy	Unhappy	Unsure	Useless
Vulnerable	Weary	Worried	

Part 2

STUBBORN STAINS:

BARRIERS TO ACTION

WHAT IS STOPPING YOU?

Focus on your potential instead of your limitations.
—Alan Loy McGinnis

For so many, it is natural to create excuses rather than face a challenge head on. But excuses are toxic; they sabotage your potential, and you need to cleanse them from your life. It is time to suck it up and focus on all the reasons why you should work for your wishes. The end result will be far more satisfying.

Excuses can be the most destructive barriers to positive action. While the list of excuses is long, we will focus on the following:

- arrogance
- codependency
- drama
- envy and comparison

- fear
- gossip and criticism
- grief
- habits and patterns
- labels
- unforgiveness
- pet peeves and complaints
- procrastination
- stress

Arrogance

Arrogance—an attitude of superiority manifested in an over-bearing manner or in presumptuous claims or assumptions (*Merriam-Webster*).

When you focus on yourself from a superficial perspective or think you or your situation is superior, you separate yourself from others—and not in a good way. An arrogant attitude is negative and damaging, and its consequences may come back to you in some way, in which case, oblivious to your own behavior, you will likely find someone or something else to blame. Sometimes it takes bravery to let people like this know how they are behaving.

We are all human beings on this planet together. No one person is better than another, so do not waste energy on that misconception. What differentiates us are the choices we make and the choices we allow others to make for us.

Codependency

Codependency—a psychological condition or a relationship in which a person is controlled or manipulated by another who is affected with a pathological condition; dependence on the needs of or control by another (*Merriam-Webster*).

I describe *codependency* as when two or more people are, by all appearances, working toward the same outcome. However, the motivations behind what they are striving for may be different. Because they are likely driven by different motivators, they likely also have different levels of commitment; chances are high that they will both fail to achieve the desired outcome.

Remember, your journey is yours alone. If you truly want to have success, you need to own it from within and not depend on someone else. Do not get me wrong—it is great to have people in your corner to support you; however, make sure it is not codependency in disguise.

You need to help yourself before you can help others. Make sure you have a very clear vision of what you are striving for and why. Otherwise, you will repeat the same self-sabotaging cycles.

Drama

Drama—a state, situation, or series of events involving interesting or intense conflict of forces . . .; dramatic state, effect, or quality (*Merriam-Webster*).

People who live their lives in constant drama often do not even realize it, but those of us who are exposed to it sure do! These individuals create drama out of any situation, sometimes even exaggerating to the point where truth is completely lost. They need to tell long, dramatic stories to draw the attention and focus of others.

By using drama as a coping method, you in essence attract more dramatic situations to your life. All that drama then buries your core issue. The question is, Why are you using drama? What are you covering up? What are you hiding from?

Envy and Comparison

Envy—painful or resentful awareness of an advantage enjoyed by another joined with a desire to possess the same advantage (*Merriam-Webster*).

Comparison—the representing of one thing or person as similar to or like another; an examination of two or more items to establish similarities and dissimilarities (*Merriam-Webster*).

Envy and comparison sometimes intertwine with arrogance and drama. Individuals struggling with these barriers often feel a pressing need to . . .

- be sicker than others (even if others have had the exact same illness)

- grieve better than others (as if others have not experienced grief themselves)

- be smarter than others (how dare you question their rightness)

- express love better than others
- give better and more than others (and are happy to tell you how much they gave or what they did)
- have better jobs than others
- suffer more and worse inconveniences than others (as though they know everything about everyone)
- be more religious than others (as though people in other religions are wrong in their beliefs or not as good of human beings as you)
- look better than others (as though everyone shows beauty in the same way)
- have more material items than others (which may mean more debt than those with fewer material items) and so on.

Take a long, hard look at yourself. You should not feel the need to outdo or be better than others. We all have our own stories, wishes, and aspirations.

Fear

Fear—an unpleasant often strong emotion caused by anticipation or awareness of danger; anxious concern (*Merriam-Webster*).

> *Do you really want to look back on your life and see how wonderful it could have been had you not been afraid to live it?*
> —*Caroline Myss*

The thing holding most people back in life is one four-letter word: *fear*. Fear of embarrassing yourself or damaging your image. Fear of imposing on others. Fear of vulnerability, failing, and so on.

Fear causes resistance and hesitation; it blocks you from possibilities. But you can overcome fear by identifying the cause and taking action against it. Focus on preparation and education. If you can, also try to find a way to have fun while you are tackling it. Show fear that it is not going to win, that it will no longer hold power over you.

Do not assume others are waiting for you to fail or embarrass yourself. In general, most people just want you to be genuine and have confidence in your actions and yourself. Assume positive intent; accept that people are ready and willing to support you.

⫸ DISCOVERY EXERCISE ⫷

If you work at figuring out where your fear is coming from, you will be able to stop the cycle. Answer the following questions to identify the source of your fear.

- Is it your go-to pattern of response to something you are not sure of?

- Is it from insecurity?

- Is it from lack of information?

- Is it from a past negative experience?

- Is it from actual danger?

If you can recognize fear surfacing, you can pause, acknowledge it, and replace it with a positive plan of action. Eventually, you will learn to catch it before it even has a chance to set in. The more you practice this, the sooner you will be able to stop it, until one day you realize you are no longer living in fear. That is freedom on a whole different level.

⇛ DISCOVERY EXERCISE ⇚

Visualization is another helpful method to utilize when facing fear.

1. Think of a task or situation that causes you fear.

2. Write down *everything* you can about it. Do not hold back—get it out.

3. Reflect. What other feelings are coming through? What can you do to remove or alleviate the source of your fear?

Example: Public Speaking

Be prepared and practice. Consider possible questions or challenges that could arise. Have something small in your pocket that makes you feel calm or reminds you to be strong—know it is there. Meditate before you begin and ask for guidance and courage. Breathe and pay attention to your audience; they will guide you.

Example: Difficult Conversation

Write down what you would actually say to that person when it is time to have that conversation, and be prepared for any scenarios that may come up. Then visualize having the actual conversation, and note what feelings come up during that exercise as well. Process them and prepare your response.

Sometimes what you feel is more extreme than fear; it is a phobia.

I used to have a phobia of water. When I would share this with others, they would tell me to just jump in and learn to swim. I had to help them understand that swimming was not the problem; I could not even wet my face in the shower without feeling strong anxiety.

I so wished to be able to be in the water, as it always looked so fun; it would also be a great fitness option. It made me sad to miss out on so many fun water activities.

At the age of fifty, I finally decided enough was enough. I was ready to kick my phobia to the curb. In my community bulletin,

I saw an aquatics schedule offering private swim lessons. It was time to take the plunge.

I called, talked to an instructor, and set up my first lesson. Then I bought a new swimsuit—half the battle, as that process is a practice in courage itself. Miraculously, I found one I loved. Another key factor that helped me prepare was all the work I had done over the past couple of years connecting with my chakras, my animal totems, and all the messages, signs, and symbols of courage and strength from my Guides (refer to "Spiritual Cleansers: Using What the Universe Reveals").

Before I left for my lesson, I went into meditation and summoned all these spiritual elements, one by one. I asked that they all gather their energy inside me to help me push through and defeat this fear that had held me hostage for most of my life. I made it clear I was ready—there was no other option but fearlessness—and off I went.

After several lessons, I am now very happy to say I can do some basic swimming and even put my head underwater. I won. Fear lost. What an amazing feeling!

Facing your fears will allow you to push them back when they try to take over in the future. Part of breaking through fear is about breaking through patterns. You just have to keep doing it—replace fear with preparation and positive action.

I recently spoke with someone about how, at age forty-five, she was starting to contemplate her life. She shared a story of her husband and his *midlife crisis*. I have heard almost every person I know over the age of forty start referencing this phase or attitude.

The conversation got me thinking. *Crisis* has such a daunting feel. It is a word people associate with fear, panic, and chaos. This is actually just another place where fear likes to rear its ugly head. So, here is my suggestion: rather than a *crisis,* instead refer to it as an *awakening.*

Awakening—a rousing from inactivity or indifference; a revival of interest in something . . .; a coming into awareness (*Merriam-Webster*).

Say you wake up one day in your forties or fifties and think, *Damn, I am in the last half of my life!*

How do you know it is your last *half* and not your last year—or even your last day? None of us are guaranteed a tomorrow. Think about that. Why are you choosing *someday* over *today?*

For those entering traditional middle age (or greater), reject the mind-set that your life is ending; you are simply entering a new phase of living. No matter your age, if you can do things that bring you joy now, do them.

I am not suggesting you shrug off your responsibilities or stop planning for a financially secure future. I *am* encouraging you to stop focusing on past regrets (could have, would have, should have). Be grateful for what you do have, and be open to your possibilities.

⫸ DISCOVERY EXERCISE ⫷

What has triggered your midlife awakening?

- Fear of realizing your mortality?
- Fear of not having what you wanted to have by now?
- Fear of not having done the things you wanted to do by now?
- Fear of not leaving the legacy you had hoped?
- Fear of not living the life you wished for yourself?

Awakening is powerful. Channel your energy toward the things that bring you joy, that make you your best you *today*. Living your best life will help others live theirs.

Gossip and Criticism

Gossip—a person who habitually reveals personal or sensational facts about others; rumor or report of an intimate nature; a chatty talk (*Merriam-Webster*).

Criticism—a critical observation or remark (*Merriam-Webster*).

> *As long as you keep a person down, some part of you has to be down there to hold him down, so it means you cannot soar as you otherwise might.*
>
> —*Marian Anderson*

Gossip and criticism are indicators of an unhealthy spirit. This type of behavior is very hurtful even if its targets remain unaware. Regardless, the Universe knows. One word: *karma*.

Karma—such a force considered as affecting the events of one's life (*Merriam-Webster*).

Gossiping about and criticizing others, especially on a regular basis, is often a coping mechanism for one's own insecurities and low self-esteem. People who do this are comforted by cutting down others to make themselves look or feel better. For some, the behavior becomes so ingrained that they may not even realize they are doing it; however, there are many others who are perfectly aware of their behavior.

Whenever you hear gossip or criticism, you have the power to say something—that is a choice you have to make (but do not do so in a way that attacks or it may backfire). If you are a participant in this behavior, chances are other gossipers/criticizers are saying things about you as well.

⫸ DISCOVERY EXERCISE ⫷

Are you a participant or a defender?

- How would you feel if someone were gossiping about or criticizing you? Would you want someone to speak up on your behalf?

> • Do you gossip or criticize others? If so, why?
> Reflect on what is really going on inside you.
> Do not direct your negativity onto others.

People need to focus on themselves and look at themselves in the mirror. Nobody is perfect. We are all struggling or suffering in some way—it is just that some know it and others do not. Be nice to yourself *and* others.

Grief

Grief—deep and poignant distress caused by or as if by bereavement [the death of a loved one]; a cause of such suffering (*Merriam-Webster*).

Grief is most often experienced following the death of a person or pet, the end of a friendship or relationship, or a major change in life circumstances.

I think many people are deeply afraid of death and use that fear to refrain from truly engaging in their life. Grief following a death can be especially paralyzing.

I experienced intense grief after the passing of my father over twenty years ago. I had attended the funerals of other loved ones, but nothing compared to losing my dad. After his passing, my spiritual encounters and experiences really intensified. It was as if my spiritual awakening was triggered through his passing. Because of this, the whole process of his death actually felt miraculous and a bit surreal.

Even though he had been ill and suffering for many years, his death was still a shock. Looking back, it was clear his time was approaching but, thankfully, we did not see that sequence as it was happening. It is one experience among many that have validated my belief in a higher power at work. I love getting signs from my dad—they make me smile, and I always say hello.

Grief is unique for each person. I do not presume the following suggestions will be appropriate for every situation, but they may provide another way of working through it.

- *Death of a loved one:* Whenever you think of that person in the future, take the time to say hello. Acknowledge what you loved about them and what you learned from them. Think of the good memories, and feel blessed to have had that person in your life for the time that you did. If they were a negative force in your life, try to use this time to reflect on the experience and release that energy.

- *End of a relationship:* Be grateful for the time you had with that person. If someone existed in your life who was toxic to you, it is still important to recognize what you learned from that relationship and then release that person and that person's energy. People are brought into our lives for a reason, no matter the duration—whether a lifetime or a single moment.

- *Major life change:* People adapt to change differently. Learn all you can about the change taking place. Accept it for what it is, especially if it is out of your control, and learn how to make a new, positive reality.

Each moment of every day is a cycle of life, death, and rebirth. From that mind-set, life does not seem so daunting or overwhelming . . . take it one moment at a time. Allow yourself to grieve what is no longer, processing all you learned from what had been, and then release that energy. It is always important to acknowledge how you feel, but never let negativity stick around to sabotage what could be something good.

Habits and Patterns

Habit—a settled tendency or usual manner of behavior; an acquired mode of behavior that has become nearly or completely involuntary (*Merriam-Webster*).

Pattern—a form or model proposed for imitation; a reliable sample of traits, acts, tendencies, or other observable characteristics of a person, group, or institution; frequent or widespread incidence (*Merriam-Webster*).

Habits and patterns form our comfort zones, and many are masters at staying within that space. All the elements discussed in this book are meant to assist you in breaking out of that beloved space. The discovery exercises will help you change your mind-set and find the strength and courage you need to do so. Once you begin to see your own habits and patterns, go ahead and assign yourself homework challenging that comfort zone. The spiritual elements discussed in later chapters may also help guide you.

Habits and patterns come in all shapes and sizes, and their origins are unique from individual to individual.

One (small) pattern I needed to change was the expectation that a person only works during the day. After receiving numerous signs and symbols involving creatures that, due to sensory characteristics, are comfortable at night (owls, cats, bats, etc.), my restless nights finally made sense: I needed to be open to working during the evening or nighttime, which is when my brain is most often firing thoughts and ideas. Instead of lying there and thinking about all these things, I had to get up and either write them all down or get on the laptop. As I like to write, more often than not, I would just scribble my notes on the notepad by my bed.

I had to accept that I may need to function differently and not try to conform to the normal schedule that most other people live by. If I am hit with an idea or creative thought during the night, I just go with it; I can always nap or sleep later.

It also became very apparent that I needed to break the routine of my life and get out of the daily rut of expectations. Working from home, it sometimes became necessary to find other times and places to do my writing and creating versus keeping myself closed off in my living space. As I am an introvert, it has been important to very often get out of my comfort zone and put myself out there—meet new people, go places by myself, do things I enjoy, talk about my work, network, and so on.

>>> **DISCOVERY EXERCISE** <<<

Write down all areas in your life where you have habits and patterns, not just with yourself but also related to others.

- What is your routine?
- Is your routine working for you?
- What is not working for you?
- Describe your comfort zone?
- Where do you feel uncomfortable?
- What homework can you give yourself to break out of it?

Pushing yourself may feel uncomfortable at first, but it does get easier.

Man's mind, once stretched by a new idea, never regains its original dimensions.

—*Oliver Wendell Holmes*

Labels

Label—descriptive or identifying word or phrase (*Merriam-Webster*).

We are a society dependent on labels: educated, uneducated; rich, poor, middle class; gay, lesbian, bisexual, transgender; autistic, mentally disabled, physically disabled; spatially challenged (overweight, skinny, short, tall); pretty, plain, ugly; employed, unemployed; mean, nice; Christian, Muslim, Jewish, Buddhist (and every other religious segment); Caucasian, African American, Indian (and any other ethnic group). These are just a few. Unfortunately, the list of labels could go on and on.

I realize there are instances where certain labels may be appropriate or necessary, but, in general, the only label that should truly mean anything is *good human being*.

Labels allow us to focus on people's differences, which causes conflict and competition. It is not surprising that many people have some level of low self-esteem or depression from being under the influence of labels.

We need to focus on how we are similar and stop focusing on how we are different. Be the person who makes the effort to meet others. Get to know who they are, understand what makes them special and unique, and determine how you can help them on their journey (and how they may be able to help you).

The best way to teach others is to lead by example. If you have issues or misunderstandings with a certain person or population group, spend some time getting to know them better. Understand their background—engage, support, and be compassionate versus ignoring, judging, and being hurtful. Getting to know others should be the norm, not the exception.

Unforgiveness

Unforgiving—having or making no allowance for error or weakness (*Merriam-Webster*).

Forgive—to stop feeling anger toward (someone who has done something wrong); to stop blaming (someone) (*Merriam-Webster*).

We can be so hard on ourselves and others. Not forgiving someone is a form of attachment. Do not let that negative residual energy of that person, situation, or event live on in you . . . let it go!

You cannot be happy or joyful while being hateful, vengeful, or afraid. You are only hurting yourself by holding on to things that happened in the past, whether yesterday or years ago.

⫸ DISCOVERY EXERCISE ⫷

Time to forgive.

- Is there anyone you need to ask to forgive you? If you do not have the opportunity to ask someone to forgive you for a wrong, then give yourself permission to forgive yourself . . . and release it.

- Is there someone you need to forgive? If someone does not ask you for your forgiveness for a wrong they may have done, forgive them anyway . . . and release it.

Yes, it may be easier said than done, especially in tragic situations, but be open to it—for yourself and your inner peace. It takes great strength and courage to forgive . . . strength and courage we do not even realize we have, but it is there, within. Releasing what is no longer serving you provides you with an incredible feeling of freedom and liberation.

Pet Peeves and Complaints

Pet peeve—a frequent subject of complaint (*Merriam-Webster*).

Complaint—an expression of grief, pain, or dissatisfaction; a formal allegation against a party (*Merriam-Webster*).

People who are constantly irritated by or complain about this, that, or the other are likely oblivious to the fact they are the source of someone else's pet peeves. We all get irritated by others or situations just as others get irritated by us.

⋙ DISCOVERY EXERCISE ⋘

What bothers you? Over the course of two weeks, write down everything, when it happens, that you consider a pet peeve or irritation.

- Why do you think it bothers you?

- How does it make you feel?

- Is it really going to impact your life now, an

> hour from now, a week from now, or even a
> year from now?
>
> ● Write down how you can turn the situa-
>   tion into a positive. Do this every time, and
>   eventually, you will stop giving energy to
>   those irritations.

Put it in perspective, and let it go! Do not give these irritations power or let them impact your own behavior in a negative way—they will just drain your energy. You may be surprised where the root of the irritation lies . . . maybe more homework will be necessary.

Procrastination

Procrastination—to put off something intentionally and habitually (*Merriam-Webster*).

> *Even if you're on the right track, you'll get run over if you just sit there.*
>
> —*Will Rogers*

Procrastination is one of the biggest excuses next to fear. Many people love procrastinating, and I have done it myself many times! Also, many who procrastinate know they do this; it is no surprise to them.

⋙ DISCOVERY EXERCISE ⋘

Why do you procrastinate? Reflect on possible reasons.

- Are you waiting for inspiration to hit?

- Are you waiting for the right resources?

- Are you waiting until "the moment is right" (after a big life event, once your vacation ends, as soon as it stops raining, after weight loss, when you are not so tired, etc.)?

- Do you think you work better under pressure?

- Do you dislike being told when to have something done?

- Do you have anyone to hold you accountable?

- Do you feel the project is unnecessary?

- Are you unsure of how to do the project?

Stress

Stress—a physical, chemical, or emotional factor that causes bodily or mental tension and may be a factor in disease causation (*Merriam-Webster*).

With the world seeming to move faster and faster, you likely suffer from occasional and sometimes even chronic stress—different kinds, different intensities, different reasons, and different coping mechanisms.

The effects of stress can show up in many ways: headaches, stomach ailments, muscle strain, fatigue, loss of focus, mood swings, disengaging from events, not participating in things you have in the past, and the list goes on.

Are you always chasing, trying to keep up, or thinking, *Someday . . .* or *When I . . .?* The saddest thing about that stress is it keeps you from being present, from being at your full potential. Stress keeps your true self hidden and beaten down.

Stress happens because you have not done the homework on yourself, and so you are in constant conflict with yourself. The natural first response is to beat yourself up for allowing stress and self-inflicted anxiety to have control over you. For example, you can be excellent at what you do, yet, if you get one small piece of negative feedback, you go crazy obsessing over that one little thing instead of all the great things you do.

Hopefully, you realize your situation before stress causes extensive damage physically or emotionally, but it is never too late to take yourself back and heal—and it is totally OK to ask for help and healing at any time. You hold that power.

ESSENTIAL CLEANSING PRODUCTS

If you want others to be happy, practice compassion. If you want to be happy, practice compassion.

—*Dalai Lama XIV*

Compassion

Compassion—sympathetic consciousness of others' distress together with a desire to alleviate it (*Merriam-Webster*).

Compassion . . . it is not about you; it is about others. Compassion is about giving someone a hug through sharing kindness and understanding and, yes, maybe even an actual hug. It is about wishing someone healing and happiness, whether verbally or silently—the same things you want for yourself. It can even be as simple as just smiling and saying hello to a stranger passing by; it may be the only smile and hello they get that day (or even longer).

LIFE CLEANSING

While traveling in a southern city, I made a stop at a general store. I had made my purchase and was standing near the door waiting for my friends. As I was standing there, a man was leaving, and as he walked by, I smiled at him and said hello (which I usually do when crossing paths with people), and he continued to exit. Just moments later, the man walked back into the store and thanked me for smiling and saying hello; he said people usually do not do that. Such a simple act, and it did not cost a thing. I believe we both walked a little taller and lighter after that exchange.

> *There are hundreds of languages in the world, but a smile speaks them all.*
>
> *—Anonymous*

Have you ever walked into a place of business or even a social venue where not one person smiled at you or acknowledged your presence? How did that make you feel? Not very good, I would guess—maybe even sad or irritated. Now, reverse the roles and think about how many times you have ignored others.

Remember: you may not know what other people are going through, just as they may not know about something you are going through. People have their own perspectives and filters. You cannot control those, which is why it is so important to keep your own mind open and refrain from judging others.

Some people always appear to be negative. Negativity is its own form of suffering, and you do not know what is causing them to live in that mind-set. Other people are really good at hiding within themselves. I suffered from stress and depression that went unnoticed for many years because, on the surface, I seemed happy, confident, self-motivated, and carefree. In reality, I was a mess inside, and I was hurting. I kept it to myself, as I did not want to burden anyone with my feelings.

Do not form assumptions based on a person's exterior appearance and actions. Always enter conversations with a foundation of compassion. If you are strong in yourself, you may intuitively feel or observe something about a person. Trust your intuition. Weave the conversation in a way that may provide you with insight; perhaps they will share what they are feeling or going through. *Listen!*

Remember, the Universe is always working through you, and you are on that person's path for a reason. You have been chosen because you have something important to give them, as they do you. Every interaction is an opportunity to impact those around us. Never underestimate the power of your impact, whether direct or indirect.

It is the nicest feeling to hear a person describe a time when something you said or did had a positive, inspiring impact on their life. That *something* could have been the littlest thing; you may not even remember saying or doing it. Maybe you included them in an activity or invited them to join you at your table. Perhaps you observed something that triggered you to approach them and start a conversation, either with the hope they would share their thoughts or with the intention of taking their mind off something troubling them.

You can impact others simply by how you carry or present yourself in various environments: professional, social, or in general. Do you present your best self? Whether you think so or not, people are always observing, judging, and making assumptions. Simply smiling, saying hello, or holding a door can make a difference to someone. Sometimes it makes a person's day or changes their mood from sad to joyful.

Think about what you are putting out into the Universe. In a simplistic way, what you give is returned to you. You have countless opportunities to be compassionate and bring pleasantness into someone's day. Start now!

⫸ DISCOVERY EXERCISE ⫷

Ask yourself these calibrating questions before you start your day.

- What is your attitude?
- What are your dominant thoughts?
- What are you feeling?
- What are you grateful for?
- Are you letting external factors influence your thoughts and behaviors?

Decide what you can do, before you leave, to make sure you are stepping out in positivity. Practicing this exercise daily will allow it to become a positive habit; eventually, you will not even realize you are doing it. It will be part of you . . . and you will know what it means to live in compassion.

Happiness cannot be traveled to, owned, earned, worn, or consumed. Happiness is the spiritual experience of living every minute with love, grace, and gratitude.

—*Denis Waitley*

Gratitude

Grateful—appreciative of benefits received; affording pleasure or contentment; pleasing by reason of comfort supplied or discomfort alleviated (*Merriam-Webster*).

Gratitude is essential for *everyone!* Every moment of your day, of your life, should be filled with gratitude. Stop complaining about what you lack, envying what other people have, and focusing on all the reasons you cannot accomplish your wishes. Instead, express daily gratitude for everything you do have.

⋙ DISCOVERY EXERCISE ⋘

Write down all you are grateful for. Do not just focus on the obvious; look at every aspect of your life. Remember to also be grateful for all the people who help make those things possible. You do not have to express gratitude for an all-inclusive list, or even the same things, every day. Sometimes gratitude can feel more genuine when it is generated by something unexpected . . . pause and acknowledge it. Following are some examples to help get you started, but the list is infinite.

I am grateful for . . .

- my home
- all the items that make my home comfortable
- indoor plumbing
- accessible drinking water
- abundance of food
- appliances to make my life easier
- access to transportation
- my human body and all its functions
- feeling the warmth of the sun
- hearing birds sing
- observing an act of kindness, and so on.

Every moment is an opportunity to learn something about yourself or someone else if you are open to recognizing it. Approaching the world from a place of learning, compassion, and gratitude will automatically guard you against negative thoughts. Without a positive perspective, that negative energy can otherwise weigh you down, harming your attitude and greater potential.

When you learn, teach. When you get, give.
—Maya Angelou

Engaging in life involves both giving and receiving.

When You Learn, Teach . . .

Following are some ways you can not only learn from others but also teach others.

- Education: You have learned interesting information or skills. You can use those to improve the skills and expand the knowledge of others, perhaps by helping someone make a career choice.

- Life lessons: You have tried different ways of tackling a problem or challenge and either failed or succeeded. You can share those lessons with others who may encounter or are going through a similar experience.

- Work or career: You have been given opportunities for professional development, advancement, or change. You can share those lessons learned and processes used to expand on those opportunities, perhaps by hosting seminars or networking events.

- Hobbies or personal interests: You have hidden talents and expertise. You can share tips and tricks with others who have similar interests, perhaps by conducting classes, hosting roundtable events, or participating in local workshops.

When You Get, Give . . .

Following are some ways you can share to help others and also how you can benefit from what others share with you.

- Financial resources: If you earn money and can spare any amount, it is always worth donating to others who may benefit.

- Time: When you have time available, whether freely or through active prioritization, your efforts and energy can always be helpful to others.

- Opportunities: If you have a positive opportunity you are able to provide to someone else, offer it together with telling that person why you think it is a good fit. Also, if a positive opportunity presents itself to you—no matter the form—give yourself permission to at least consider it if not take it fully. Do not allow yourself to look back and regret not doing something when you had the chance.

Be open and listen to what others are saying in conversation. Sometimes you will be the learner, and sometimes you will be the teacher. It should feel great to be both. It is important to avoid an arrogant, know-it-all mind-set. Stay humble.

This sharing has no limitations; an adult can learn from a child just as much as an adult can teach a child. There should never be boundaries or restrictions to learn and teach—everyone benefits.

You can likely recall a time when you received something unexpectedly and how great it felt, how it warmed your heart even if for a short moment. You can also likely recall a time when you gave something to someone, openly or anonymously, and how good that made you feel.

The joy of giving and receiving is a natural high. Be grateful for all you learn, and be grateful for all you are able to teach. Be grateful for all you receive, and be grateful for all you are able to give.

Put good out into the Universe, and it will come back to you.

LETTING GO: WHAT, WHY, WHEN, HOW

The meaning of things lies not in the things themselves, but in our attitude towards them.

—*Antoine de Saint-Exupéry*

It is often a difficult struggle to let go of attachments, whether physical or emotional. Those things have become comfortable to you; that is perfectly natural. However, the attachments you consume and bring into your life can sometimes turn around and consume you.

Physical/Material Attachments

People often underestimate the underlying work necessary before letting go can begin. Attachment, or clutter, relates to more than overflowing drawers, closets, or rooms; it also relates to your inner self. Everything is connected to your feelings. To successfully detach, you need to identify and work through internal feelings and motivators. Yes, you can have someone help you get rid of the "stuff," but that will not change your future behavior. You must first understand the reasons behind the attachment. This is a powerful process!

⋙ DISCOVERY EXERCISE ⋘

Think about everything you have in your home. Reflect on these questions while doing so.

- Why do you have it?

- What value does it bring you?

- How does it make you feel?

- Does it support your wishes, what you want your life to be, what is important in life?

- How would you feel if you were asked to let it go?

- Do you feel a lot of anxiety when your possessions are threatened? If so, what do you think is at the root of that feeling? What is the trigger?

- What happened at about the time you started the behavior of accumulating clutter? That is likely where you need to start cleansing.

Control is often used as a coping mechanism. You are in control of the things you bring into your life, so you may interpret letting go of those items as losing control. That can lead to a great amount of stress, which flows over into other areas of your life. Again, this concerns more than just physical possessions.

⇝ DISCOVERY EXERCISE ⇜

When you feel the need to acquire something, ask yourself these questions.

- What is going on in your life that makes you want to purchase it?

- What is it about that item that draws you to it?

- Is it the thrill of the purchase, or is it just because you can?

- Do you think it will bring you long-term happiness? Why?

- Does it have a purpose/use? Does it have more than one?

- Do you have space for it?

- Does it meet the needs of any of your wishes?

- Does it fit into what you want your life to be?

> Please know I am not saying you should avoid purchasing or keeping anything—just put some thought into the reason *why* you are purchasing an item or keeping it in your life.

As I lay in bed one morning, I looked around the room and thought about all the stuff I had. Though it was not much—I happen to be a purger—I realized I did not have any true attachment to any of it. I could literally pack a suitcase with some clothing and essentials, my laptop and phone, and hit the road. All my other belongings could be given to family and friends, sold, or donated, and my critical documents could always be kept in a secure location.

This was a profound realization: I had, over time, purged away all the excess in my life and kept only what I considered special or truly needed and used. Much of what I still had were small, sentimental things I could pass on to other family members. After that, all I would have left would be large numbers of photos and other memorabilia, but I could scan or photograph all of that, save it digitally, and pass the physical items to family if appropriate. When I finished thinking through this, I felt an immense sense of release and freedom!

Questioning the possessions you bring into your life is a concept of minimalism. Do not buy something just because those around you, or society in general, push you to do so.

Purchase it because you need it and it brings value to your life. (However, be careful not to equate possessions with success or status. The short-term feeling of fulfillment will ultimately disappear, and you will someday wake up feeling suffocated by all the stuff—and possibly debt—weighing you down.)

Some of you may now be asking, "But what about my collection of _____?" To collect or not to collect . . . that is a very tough question.

It is amazing how collections can spiral out of control. Perhaps it started with a single knickknack bought as a souvenir (e.g., a bell, spoon, shot glass). Maybe someone bought you a gift and encouraged you to start a collection, or maybe it started with a love of reading. Suddenly, others felt they needed to add to your collection—and now, years later, it numbers in the dozens or even hundreds. You realize it has overtaken your physical space and wonder why you ever let it reach this point. You may not even like that item or theme anymore!

Perhaps reality only hits once it is time for you to move or downsize; you have to either pack it all up piece by piece, keep just a few special items, or sell and donate the whole works, as nobody you know wants any of it.

Sound familiar? So, what do you do?

⋙ **DISCOVERY EXERCISE** ⋘

It is time to deal with your collection, whatever it may be.

1. Be honest about how looking at the whole collection, in one space, makes you feel. If some of the items were gifts, you may feel obligated to keep them because you do not want to make anyone feel bad. But if it does not fill you up with joy, it is time to let it go. This is about you, not anyone else!

2. Really dig into your feelings about each item. Use the questions provided in the previous two exercises as a guide. Determine whether it adds long-term value to your life.

3. If you have decided the space is too small or cluttered, or you want to use the occupied space for something else, focus on the future. Have a clear picture of what you want the end result to be, how you want it to function, and how it will make you feel. That visualization and feeling will help you through the process of letting go.

4. Start with the easy or obvious: do a first pass, taking out all items you can toss (i.e., broken or damaged).

Determine if any of them are of high value and can be sold. Then decide if any can be donated.

5. Look at each remaining item and decide if you really want or need to keep it. At this point, everything should be in one of four piles: keep, toss, sell, or donate. For the items you plan to sell, set a one-week deadline to get them advertised. Give yourself an additional week or two to sell them—keep things moving.

6. Once you have cleared out the space(s), do a deep clean. Follow through on your vision of what you want the space to be.

7. Congratulate yourself on going through this process and achieving your vision. Chances are you will be motivated to take on additional projects. Your family and friends may even start asking you to teach them how to do it.

Emotional Attachments

While most of this chapter concerns physical attachments, the same concepts can relate to nonphysical aspects of your life. You can apply many of the same exercise questions to emotional baggage. This may involve destructive relationships, negative experiences from the past, converting from a negative attitude to a positive attitude, replacing ineffective emotions with new perspectives, and so on.

In many cases, the physical items in your life are connected to emotional attachments.

You may find, after you go through the discovery exercises earlier in this chapter, that the emotional aspects will be cleansed and fall away. This can be a very intense process. Give it time, honor it, and respect it.

Time to Release

When you reach the point where you are ready to let go of attachments (large or small, physical or emotional), have a "release session." Take the time to be grateful and thank the Universe for all it has provided and to support you in letting those things go. Appreciate the ability to help others benefit from what you no longer need or use; express your willingness to let it go.

Cleansing your life of physical and emotional clutter allows you to immerse yourself, wherever you are, in whatever you are doing. Life is a precious gift, so do everything you can to be present. Use your senses to experience the people, nature, architecture, and animals around you. Listen to the stories, histories, and experiences of others. Remember, *things* are not what is important—it is living a full life, exploring, experiencing, and connecting with people.

Part 3

SPIRITUAL CLEANSERS: USING WHAT THE UNIVERSE REVEALS

WHAT THIS "UNIVERSE" STUFF IS ALL ABOUT

We are divine enough to ask and we are important enough to receive.

—*Wayne Dyer*

I refer to *the Universe* as a quick way to describe the unexplainable, those things that reveal themselves to you in ways you cannot fully understand. I am not here to explain *how* the Universe works; I am here to describe the amazing things I have experienced, how they have helped me, and how they have guided me to transform not only myself but also my life.

Everything you receive, good and bad, is a gift; it is all about perspective. You may need to work hard to keep yourself open to receiving. This is not always easy; there will likely be times when you are just plain exhausted from all the homework and the need to be constantly in the present. You may catch yourself falling into old habits and patterns that no longer serve you, in which case, you will have to work your way back out again. But it does get easier the closer you get to achieving your desired change or realizing your true self and higher purpose. There is always change around the corner, just waiting for you to be aware and to see where it leads you.

It is exciting that more and more people are becoming open to and accepting of the topic of intuition and psychic abilities. For many years, I did not share what I was experiencing with others apart from a few people I knew were open to it. You can usually tell when someone is not comfortable with the discussion by their body language. As I have continued to develop my abilities and own my purpose, I no longer shy away from sharing my experiences. They are all part of who I am. You will know when you have reached that level of validation for yourself.

Connecting with the Universe simply starts with being open and observant. Be intentional with your thoughts, with what you are putting out into the Universe, so it knows what to give you in return. It is not just about asking for specific things; it is also about asking to have the right people and opportunities placed on your path. Then, when they do show up, you must not only recognize them but accept them. You also need to trust what your intuition is telling you to do with the Universe's gifts. Every person, every interaction, and every vibe we get is for a reason.

If you stop and really think about it, every single person is blessed in dozens, maybe even hundreds, of ways every single day! The question is whether they are paying attention. I am guessing not many are . . . or at least not as much as they could be.

⋙ DISCOVERY EXERCISE ⋘

Following are questions you can ask to help you connect with the Universe. As this is a long list, perhaps choose just three of them each day. Write down your responses and take time to reflect on them at the end of your day.

- What happened to you today? Why do you think those things happened?

- How are you feeling? Why are you feeling that way? Do you need to make adjustments?

- Did you wish love, kindness, compassion, good health, and healing to others who crossed your path?

- Did you do something kind for someone? Did someone do something kind for you? If so, did you sincerely thank them?

- Why do you think you are crossing paths with a person? What are you meant to learn from that person? What is that person meant to learn from you?

- Is something being revealed to or about you? Were you taught a lesson?

- Did something happen to move you closer to one of your wishes? Was a wish met?

- Did you spend time in nature? What did you do? How did you feel?

- Did you look up at the sky? What did you see? How did you feel?

- Did you express gratitude throughout the day?

After all that, you cannot tell me you had a boring day or did not learn anything today!

In the following chapters, we will cover birth codes, signs and symbols, spirit animals and animal totems, spirits and Guides, your inner child, past lives, the many layers of dreams, vision quests, vibes, chakras, and meditation.

The following chapters also relay many of my own spiritual experiences, elements, perspectives, and learnings regarding the above areas. As my focus is to offer a personal perspective, I do not include scientific explanations for these elements. I have had much time to understand how to interpret and utilize these elements in the *Life Cleansing* process. The examples and stories I share relate to the discovery of my own core issue and the work I needed to do to live my higher purpose.

Your examples and stories may feel similar. With that said, please do not put unnecessary pressure on yourself to have all or even some of these same experiences or to have them right away. Your journey is unique, and your experiences and interpretations may differ based on your own core issue and the work you need to do. You will tap into and experience what is meant for you when you are ready to receive it. Allow yourself time to get comfortable with the information and to open yourself to your possibilities.

I am excited to tell you that, to this day, I continue to have new and varied experiences. Learn to connect with yourself and with all that is around you. Have fun with your curiosity! So long as you keep yourself open to receiving, the Universe will continue to provide.

Now relax, breathe, and clear your mind to receive.

SPIRITUALITY OR RELIGION:
IT IS NOT A COMPETITION

When I talk to people about my work and spiritual experiences, there is one question that often comes up in the conversation: "Do you believe in God?" As you talk to people about this book and the work you are doing, you may be asked this question as well. Please note that the following is based on my own personal thoughts and opinions.

Religion is another label society places on people, and, unfortunately, it can be a great instigator of separation. As I mentioned earlier, the only label I focus on is *good human being.* In my opinion, that has nothing to do with whether or not you belong to a certain religion.

I consider myself spiritual but not religious. I believe in God as the source of our creation and as the energy of our Universe but not as the representative of any one religion.

I am comfortable saying I believe that with every facet of my being.

While I have been baptized and confirmed in a Christian religion, that does not impact who I am as a person. Christianity, as with any religion, is a philosophy based on the beliefs, interpretations, expressions, and control of others over many centuries. I believe it is more important to study all religious and spiritual philosophies versus limiting myself to one or another.

When I was a small child, I believed in God before I even knew the story of Christianity—that faith was just in me, perhaps as a result of my past lives. I have never felt comfortable going to church; however, I have always felt comfortable praying to God (the Universe) and connecting to my spirituality wherever I am. I do not need to be within the walls of a structure to show my spiritual faith. Faith resides within me and is with me all the time.

Religion and spirituality are individual choices. I have no interest in changing or influencing people to be or believe one thing or another, nor is that my right. I believe what I believe, and you believe what you believe.

So, when you are asked *the question,* know your personal beliefs and be willing to express them . . . but, as with anything, do so respectfully and with an openness to hear other perspectives.

OPENING UP: USING YOUR BIRTH CODE

Your birth code is a means of connecting to a higher dimension, to your energy and your Guides, using your date of birth. It empowers you to open yourself up to receiving.

⫸ DISCOVERY EXERCISE ⫷

Use the following steps to determine your numerical birth code (using November 6, 1992, as an example). Note: When the number has more than one digit, add those digits together to get it to one digit.

1. Write down your birth month (e.g., November). The number for November is 11.
    Month = 11 → 1 + 1 → **2**

2. Write down your birth day (e.g., 6). Day = **6**

3. Write down your birth year (e.g., 1992).
    Year = 1992 → 1+9+9+2 → 21 → 2+1 → **3**

4. Write down the above three numbers, in order, to
    see your birth code (e.g., **263**).

You have figured out your birth code, what purpose does it serve?

Resistance

You can use your birth code to break through resistance. Resistance is when you avoid, ignore, reject, or dread interacting with someone or something. Oftentimes, you know you are doing so because you likely feel tension around the person or thing; you may even have a physical reaction, such as an increased heart rate, sweating, or nausea. You are also likely to come up with many excuses to avoid the person or situation.

Guidance

You can use your birth code to open yourself to guidance in any situation. Some situations include public speaking (ask for calmness, the ability to read the audience, and effectively express your message), writing a speech (ask for the words you need to reach your audience), or attending meetings and events (ask for the ability to interact and communicate effectively).

Spiritually Active Environments

Even if you believe in spirits and have experienced them before, as I have, it can still be a little unnerving to experience them in certain places. But do not let these situations cause you fear; when you are in an environment where spirits may want to visit you, keep yourself open to them. If they do come through, thank them, ask them questions if you are comfortable doing that, and then tell them they may now move on. Do not assume spirits are out to hurt you. Really, they just want to communicate in some way, so, as you would with a physical human being, be respectful.

⋙ DISCOVERY EXERCISE ⋘

Use this exercise to open your birth code and make your statement of what you are open to receiving. You can do this anytime and anywhere; you do not have to be in a private space or sitting down—you can do this exercise walking down the street if that is what you need to do.

1. Open your posture by standing or sitting tall and not having your arms or legs crossed.

2. Take a few deep breaths to relax your mind.

3. Say your birth code followed by your statement, whether out loud or silently in your head.

4. Repeat your birth code and statement three times in a row.

Following are some examples of possible phrases to use when opening your birth code. You can use any statement you want that is relevant to you; these are just examples to help you get started.

- I am open to the people I need to meet on my journey.

- I am open to the experiences I need to help me on my journey.

- I am open to possibilities.

- I am open to my higher purpose.

- I release all that is no longer serving me.

- I am open to signs, symbols, dreams, and visits.

- I am open to the words I need. (*Be specific if you can—e.g., for a tough conversation.*)

- I allow all negative energy to pass through me completely and not stay with me. (*This is especially important if you are around or preparing to be around negative people or situations.*)

- I release all resistance and open myself to what I need.

It is natural for this to feel a bit awkward at first, but it will get easier, and you will find yourself using the practice quite often. This exercise places you into an open mind-set that allows you to receive what you need. Then you release it and let the Universe do its thing. In some ways, it takes the pressure off you. Believe and trust.

GETTING CLARITY THROUGH
SIGNS AND SYMBOLS

You may be wondering about the difference between signs and symbols. *Signs* are what you receive while awake, and *symbols* are what you receive while asleep.

Signs

Not everything you see is a sign, yet somehow, you know instinctively when you see one. Why is that? It is because your soul knows what it is looking for and alerts you when the Universe provides. It says, "Look, did you see that?"

Signs provide validation that you are on the right path. Sometimes that validation appears as reminders of certain people, places, or moments in your life. Signs can be just about anything and appear just about anywhere—on billboards and television shows; in movies, songs, and magazines; on street signs and license plates; on the ground, in the sky, on your own body . . . The list goes on.

Before you begin your day, open yourself to any signs you need to receive. It is important to look at the context around potential signs as well. Do not walk around constantly trying to turn everything into a sign; trust that you will know one when you see one. Be careful not to set expectations around the number of signs you receive. Just open yourself and let the Universe provide.

⫸ DISCOVERY EXERCISE ⫷

Over the course of two weeks, write about any signs you receive. Answer the following questions for each sign.

- What was the sign?
- Where did you see it?
- If it was an object, how many were there?
- If it was a living thing, what was it doing?
- What color was it?
- Was there a scent?
- What was the weather like?
- What were you doing when you saw it?
- What was on your mind before it appeared?

- What happened earlier that day?
- Were you missing someone?
- Were you trying to solve a problem, answer a question, or make a decision?
- What made you think it was a sign?

If a sign appears often and you feel a strong connection to it, you may want to have a physical object in your home as a reminder of its wonderful messages.

Anchors, pennies, and spiderwebs are just three of the many signs I have received.

Anchors

The anchor showed up in my life just about every way it could: television, clothing, jewelry, décor, and so on. However, there was one place it took me completely by surprise—genealogy. Out of curiosity, I looked up my family name in Scotland . . . and guess what? The prominent feature of our family crest was the anchor. The discovery gave me chills. Anchors continue to appear at different stages of my journey. As a sign, it keeps me grounded where I am until I need to move along to my next destination.

Pennies

Lots of pennies! I think many people relate to this one. Pennies started showing up in my late thirties, when I was experiencing much change in my life. They have appeared while or just before I changed my job, had a critical career discussion, or bought or sold a home. They also appear when I need reassurance on a decision, spend time with family, attend special events, and so on. One special story comes to mind in particular.

At my last job, I was responsible for organizing and executing a large sales incentive trip to Hawaii. About a week prior to our departure, the news reported not just one but two hurricanes headed for the Big Island. They were expected to make landfall at about the same time our attendees would arrive. I was in communication all week with my local contact, who repeatedly assured me it would not hit the side where we were staying. In turn, I worked hard to reassure our attendees it would be fine and to continue with their travel as planned.

When it was time for me to head out—a couple of days ahead of everyone else—I prayed to my dad during the entire ride to the airport. I asked him to let me know everything would be OK. When I got to the airport, there was no line to check my bag or pass through security. I thought that was a good sign in itself; things were going smoothly.

As I leaned over to take my laptop out of my carry-on bag for security, what was lying on the ground right by my foot? You guessed it: a shiny penny! I got the biggest smile and whispered a thank-you as I picked it up. Right then and there, I knew everything would, in fact, be OK.

One of the hurricanes did hit . . . on the other side of the island. The second veered off without making landfall. Although a few attendees were delayed, all of them made the trip. The program's events and activities were the best ever, and the trip was amazing for everyone!

I have discovered that the pennies I receive are, surprisingly, not just from my dad but from my Guides. They are a way to assure me, through the third dimension, that I am on the right path and all is well. Now, I keep every penny I find. I put them in a jar in a special area of my home so I can keep their energy together. Needless to say, I love it when I see pennies in unexpected places!

Spiderwebs

The spiderweb is just one of many Celtic symbols that have appeared throughout my journey. Spiderwebs go back to ancient times when languages were first being written. I love this sign; it provided me with great validation and courage while writing this book, and it continued to appear to me throughout the editing process. This sign was telling me to keep going with my writing; the sign represents weaving my purpose and my future.

Body Signs

Signs can also show up on the body. Injured limbs, muscle pains, digestive issues, headaches, and sinus issues . . . all of these can relate to challenges or blockages in your life and indicate where you need to focus your attention. A physical manifestation can mean you are resisting something that needs to happen, or you are not expressing your true self. This was an eye-opener for me. If you receive a body sign, take time to figure out what is going on within you; then work on getting yourself healthy again.

Signs are such special gifts to receive. Embrace them, learn their messages, and use them to guide you on your *Life Cleansing* journey.

Symbols

As with dreams, symbols often have layers, and until they are interpreted, they may not make much sense. Symbols are interesting in their own way because they represent the other-dimensional. They are unique messages given just to you.

You may be wondering how you can see a symbol if it is not of our third dimension. Personally, a symbol will come to me just as I am drifting off to sleep (that interesting in-between space between consciousness and unconsciousness) or while I am in a deep sleep. Regardless of sleep stage, my eyes will just pop open and the symbol will be there, almost like it is being projected. It will only remain for a few seconds at most, and I have learned to take in every detail of the experience.

The most important thing is to write everything down right away. Depending on how deep asleep I was before receiving the symbol, I may just write a few words to allow recall in the morning. Other times, I may write down every detail. Seeing a symbol is a great gift, so I do not like to waste it by not writing it down.

Caution: A note written in the dark—after being jolted out of a deep sleep—can be an interesting deciphering exercise come morning! There have been a few times when I had absolutely no idea what I had written; it was true scribbling.

Remember you have no control over what symbols will appear to you. Each one is unique, and often strange, but every symbol has a message.

Sometimes, a symbol will reappear at different times; however, it may be a different color, size, or brightness to indicate progress or strength. These reoccurring symbols are a reminder to reflect on their meaning again and make sure you are incorporating its positive qualities and message into your life. I actually talk to some of my reoccurring symbols; I tell them I see them and understand what they are telling me. Sometimes I just simply thank a symbol for its message.

Types

Even though each symbol is unique, they often fall into one of these categories:

- animal
- nature (e.g., flowers, plants, trees)
- color
- shape

- number
- structure (e.g., bridges, buildings, houses, rooms)
- object (e.g., chairs, ladders, bricks, rocks, clocks, gridlines)

Times and Places

As symbols typically appear during sleep, they are most likely to appear somewhere in your bedroom (on or near your wall, bed, closet door, or bedroom door); however, they can appear in any room where you are resting. Symbols do not necessarily appear every night; there may be really active weeks, and there may be quiet nights with no activity. You get what you need when you need it.

Appearances

A symbol is most often four to twenty-four inches in size, but occasionally it can take up a whole wall. It may be solid and still, or it may flash, pulse, float, or fade. Some disappear in an instant, while others remain for a few seconds.

Feelings

There are times when a symbol can generate a feeling within you, such as peace, understanding, confusion, anger, or fear. Some may just be telling you to pay attention.

Human Energies

A symbol that has human energy often has a beckoning quality to it, like it wants you to see it and follow it. These symbols are more orb-like or have a more fluid, nongeometric shape.

These symbols are always different, but their underlying energy is similar; you can just feel their humanness. (In some cases, these are actually spirit or past life visits; I will talk about these visits in a later chapter). These do not appear often, so when they do, it is a real gift. They are validating that you are open to connecting and receiving the messages you need.

To give you an idea of what symbols can look like, here are just some of my own. Be open to anything you see, no matter how strange or unexpected.

- Apples; on closet door
- Black ball with red and white dots; top of bedroom door
- Black circles joined to form an upside-down triangle; top of closet door
- Black eyes, nose, and fingers; peeking over top of bedroom door
- Black shapes (geometric or random), floating away (past life visits); top of closet door
- Blue flashing light in a tree; on wall
- Bouquet of black licorice-like strands with green-and-red paper background; top of closet door
- Brick wall with a door and red gridlines along the mortar; on whole wall
- Cloudy white disc with energy light in the center, floating away (Guide visit); on the bed

- Dahlias (one color and multicolored); top of closet door or on wall
- Drawer closing; on wall
- Holly berries; on wall
- Light green, Celtic-like pattern; on whole wall
- Light green empty wooden shelving; on wall
- Little evergreen trees flashing; on bed
- Numbers (1:11, 2:22, 3:33, 4:44, 5:55); on digital clock
- Roses, daisies, and other flowers in various colors; on wall or closet door
- Three intertwined circles; on wall
- White robe with sleeves extended out to the side; on wall

⋙ DISCOVERY EXERCISE ⋘

Over the course of two weeks, write about any symbols you receive and answer the following questions. If possible, write down the details when it actually happens, as they may fade or disappear by the time you wake up.

- What did you see?
- Was it a single object or multiple objects?

- What size was it?

- What colors were represented?

- What shapes were represented?

- Where did it appear?

- What was it doing?

- How did it make you feel?

- Did it feel like a human energy?

- What were you pondering before you fell asleep?

- Did you ask for guidance on something that day or before you went to bed?

A fun part of understanding and interpreting signs and symbols is the process of looking up their meanings. There is so much information available online and in books; all you need to do is search the various elements and read all you can. Something you may not expect as you research signs and symbols (as well as other topics) is that what pops up in your search one day may not pop up the next day. The reason for that is your own energy—if your energy is open, you will find what you need; however, if you resist the message trying to be delivered, then you may struggle to find the information you need.

When this happens to me, I leave the search alone for a couple of days. Then I go back, open my birth code, and search again . . . and, miraculously, what I need will reveal itself.

I love to receive signs and symbols. They provide so much information, and they are so interesting to research and interpret. The messages they relay, and the great *Life Cleansing* insights they provide, never cease to amaze me, especially when combined with all the other messages the Universe provides. Fascinating!

ANIMALS HAVE MUCH TO SAY—LISTEN

As you learn about and work with animal energies, you may discover yourself gaining a stronger appreciation for *all* living things. You truly can learn from anything and everything; you just have to be open. Animal qualities are a great resource in *Life Cleansing*, as they give you guidance on what to bring into your life.

Animals appear as signs and symbols, in nature, and also in our dreams. Animals cover many categories, including birds, insects, and reptiles, and they each have strong energy and meaning. However, for simplicity, I will use *animals* to represent all groups.

This chapter will cover animals in two different ways: spirit animals and animal totems. You may be a bit confused about the difference between the two. To put it simply, *animal totems* are with you through your whole life, and *spirit animals* are with you when you need help at certain points in your life.

Spirit Animals

Pay attention to the details when an animal of any type makes a noticeable and sometimes recurring appearance. It has a message for you!

⋙ DISCOVERY EXERCISE ⋘

Over the course of two weeks, be aware of any animals that appear, and answer the following questions. Animals can show up in many ways: in person, on TV, in magazines, online, and so on.

- Is this animal unusual for you to see?
- Are you seeing more of the animal than you normally do?
- What was it doing?
- How many were there?
- What color was it? Were there other colors involved?
- Where were you?
- Were others with you?
- What was the environment around it?
- What was the weather like?
- Were you interacting with it? If so, how?
- How did you feel?

Answering these questions can provide great insight and guidance for your interpretation of the experience. The spirit animal may tell you what qualities or activities you need to bring into or change in your life, or it will validate what you are already doing or utilizing.

⫸ DISCOVERY EXERCISE ⫷

After encountering a spirit animal, research the animal and understand how it applies to your life. Consider the following areas of research to study.

- Spiritual, medicine card, and cultural meanings
- Physical characteristics
- Behaviors
- Environment
- Diet
- Predators or other threats

When researching the animal, there may be questions listed that you can ask yourself to help understand the message behind why it is appearing, whether you are utilizing the positive characteristics and, if you are not using them, asking yourself why you are not.

Caution: Do not assume an animal you think of as "bad" is a bad sign. Some animals may pleasantly surprise you with their message!

While you will encounter your own spirit animals, following is a list of some of the spirit animals that have visited (and, at times, revisited) me: ants, bald eagles, bears, bees, cats, cows and bulls, dogs, elephants, horses, moose, owls, peacocks, pigs, red-tailed hawks, snakes, spiders, swans, turtles, vultures, and worms.

Another interesting facet of researching your spirit animals is discovering patterns that emerge among their qualities and messages . . . and how applicable they are to your *Life Cleansing* work.

Animal Totems

There are many theories and teachings related to determining your animal totems as well as how many you have. Research this and determine what feels right for you. My intent here is to focus on the *purpose* of animal totems.

I have three animal totems with me for life. They connect to three different areas: me, my purpose, and how I take my purpose out into the world.

- Me: Bengal tiger—fearlessness, persistence, strength, and playfulness

- My purpose: Himalayan vulture—soaring on energy fields, perception, inner and outer sight

- How I take my purpose out into the world: Alsatian
  Wolf Dog, now known as the German shepherd—tireless
  integrity, dedication, loyalty, approachability, playfulness

Trying to figure out my three animal totems was an interesting process. I had to do my homework, much of which involved digging through books on animals and focusing on wherever my energy hit, in addition to seeking guidance from my mentor. A couple of my totems were definitely not what I expected, but they are all strong, and I feel fortunate to have them with me.

Regardless of the method you use to identify your totems, the most important thing is to honor them and keep their energy active. Include them in your meditation practice, place physical representations of them in your home or special space, and see them in a natural environment if possible.

One way I represent my animal totems in my home came through tapping into my long-dormant creative self by creating artwork. This has helped me develop a stronger connection with my animal totems.

As it had been years since I drew anything, I bought a new sketch pad and drawing pencils. First, I looked online and found images of my totems. I put the images I was drawn to into a document, compared them, and selected my favorite three for each totem. Next, I converted the images to gray scale so I could better see their texture. Then I chose one photo of each to sketch.

I started and restarted my Bengal tiger a few times, but I just could not get it, so I quit. A couple of nights later, I started again, this time with the Alsatian Wolf Dog. Using a regular drawing pencil, I just went for it. Miraculously, I finished the sketch in about ten minutes. Feeling inspired, I drew the Himalayan vulture—it, too, was finished in about ten minutes. Back to the Bengal tiger. I chose a different image, cleared my head, and began; this time, it was done in about ten minutes. I could not believe I did all three sketches in only thirty minutes!

For the next part of my homework, I went to the store and energetically chose frames for the drawings. It was an interesting exercise, and I found the perfect frames. I chose background paper from old scrapbooking supplies. I hung the framed drawings on my bedroom wall, where I could see them when I went to bed at night and again in the morning when I woke. This homework helped me feel the energy of my totems and let go of the need to draw perfectly and just let the pencil flow. I have to admit they turned out great!

This project inspired me in other ways as well. I pulled out all my old drawings from my childhood and teenage years. With these, as well as my recent totem drawings, I created a photo book. It reminds me I can be creative even when I think I do not have it in me—and I am good at it. As a *Life Cleansing* exercise, this helped me break through an old pattern of thinking I could not do something unless I did it perfectly.

Understand, feel, and embrace the incredible energy and qualities of animals.

SPIRITS AND GUIDES: THEY JUST WANT TO COMMUNICATE

Is there a difference between *spirits* and *Guides?* While I have had far more experiences with spirits, I have had enough encounters with a few of my Guides to determine yes, there is.

Spirits

Spirits are fascinating, especially since they are able to communicate so much through their energy alone.

While you may have your own experiences, following is how I describe the spirits I see:

- I am able to see their body shapes, which are black in color and in a standing position but lack any identifying characteristics (facial features or body definition). However, some spirits come through as dark, translucent orbs or floating shapes (general or geometric).

- I am able to see their size, which varies to include those of adults, youths, or babies.

- I am able to feel their approximate age (through energy).

- I am able to tell if they are male or female (through energy).

- I am able to feel if it is calm, excited, sad, and the like (through energy).

You may be wondering what I did when I saw spirits for the first time. If you have ever been visited by a spirit, you may relate to my experience; if you have not, perhaps it will prepare you for when you do.

I started seeing spirits in my late twenties. The first time it happened, I was startled but not frightened. I was living in a one-bedroom apartment in the upper level of my sister's home. I was single at the time so had my room to myself. I would describe the experience as a fluid moment of awaking in the night to see a vision at the foot of my bed. It was a human shape (male energy) holding the shape of a baby.

It was a brief encounter but certainly memorable, and it reoccurred several times over the years at every place I lived. There was an emotion emanating from the man that I could not quite explain. At first, I thought it was maybe my dad with the spirit of a miscarried baby my mom had when I was a young child. However, I felt a stronger connection as time went on. I wondered if it was actually my own miscarried baby I had in my early twenties.

Fast-forward a number of years later. A woman suggested the visits were a sign I was giving, or about to give, birth to something new in my life. She also suggested, if the spirit was my baby, to name him or her so its soul could move on. The next time they appeared, I released both my chosen boy and girl names to the baby spirit (although my sense was the baby was male). Those spirits have not visited me since. The experience was very emotional, and I grieved, in a sense, as I felt a loss. I still miss seeing them appear at the end of my bed.

When I met my mentor a few years ago, that spirit encounter was still very much on my mind. I asked her who the man and baby were. She said they were actually my husband and son from a past life (AD 1582 in France) in which my baby and I died from hemorrhage during his birth. I immediately started crying. As it turned out, in that past life, I died at the same age I was in my current life when I miscarried and nearly died from extreme blood loss. This revelation was a very emotional moment for me, especially since I never went on to have any children.

While that was my most involved, lengthy, and emotional spirit encounter, I have had a number of other experiences as well. Seeing a spirit is similar to seeing a symbol—there will be a moment in the night when my eyes just pop open . . . and there they will be.

Sometimes I am startled by how close they are to me, but, again, I have never felt frightened. The experience reminds me of when I was a little girl when, if I got scared in the night, I would go into my parents' bedroom. I would stand by mom's side of the bed and just stare at her, willing her to wake until her eyes suddenly opened and she saw me. (It often freaked her out a bit—sorry, Mom.)

There have been numerous occasions when one or a couple of spirits have stood by me at the head of my bed. At each of my residences, I often got the *spirit lineup*—a line of spirits starting at the head of my bed and extending all the way down the hall. I felt like I needed one of those take-a-number dispensers to help them one by one!

At first, I had not yet understood or embraced my psychic abilities. The spirits seemed to appear more and more often when I was majorly stressed with my job, working nonstop and barely sleeping. Waking up almost nightly to those spirit lineups was adding to that exhaustion. One night, I decided I could not take it anymore. I told the spirits (through silent communication from me to them) to please go away; I needed to sleep. Once I did that, they stopped visiting.

Fast-forward again to my first meeting with my mentor. I asked her if these spirits were relatives of mine and why they were lining up like that. She told me they could be anybody; they were there because they wanted me to help them with something and to communicate with others for them. She said I could open up that ability if I wanted to. As of this book's publishing, I have not yet reopened my connection to those spirit lineups. However, exploring that possibility may be something still to come on my amazing journey.

In addition to visual sightings, following are other types of incidences involving spirits. Some may sound familiar to you.

- *A touch*: Have you ever been by yourself, or maybe even around others, and felt a touch on your cheek, hand, or hair—so light that you questioned whether you actually felt it?

- *A smell*: Have you ever been in a space by yourself and suddenly smelled the perfume or cologne or even cigarette smoke of a deceased family member? Or maybe it smelled as though someone walked by with a bouquet of fragrant flowers?

- *An interaction:* Have you ever been in a place or situation where something physical happened unexplainably, such as a light or TV turning off or on by itself, or seeing an object in a place where it had not been prior?

- *Orbs*: Have you ever taken a photograph and noticed orb-like shapes? Yes, those are spirits as well. You have to admit you get excited when you see those in your photos. Makes you wonder who is there!

A Ghost Story

While this story is true, I love to share it just for fun. Over a summer celebration weekend, I stayed at a campground with my sisters and a couple of friends in our friend's large camper. One of my sisters and I were sleeping in the bedroom while the others slept in the main part of the camper. At some point, I woke to the appearance of a spirit. But unlike others, this one was a full-color woman—I saw her skin, hair color, facial features, and clothing, and she was emerging from between my sister's head of the bed and the sidewall cabinet.

When I saw her come through by my sister, I went into protective mode and told her to get out of there. I did not think it to her as I normally would; I actually yelled out loud, waking my sister. I asked if she had heard me yell at someone to get out of there, and she said she definitely did. I apologized, and we both tried going back to sleep. Of course, I told the others all about it the next day. They freaked out just a little!

➤➤➤ DISCOVERY EXERCISE ◄◄◄

Thinking over the course of your life, especially recent years, write down any spirit encounters you have experienced. Use as much detail as possible when considering and answering the following questions. (Do not worry if you have not had experiences; not everyone is open to or experiences the same things.)

* What was going on in your life at the time of the encounter?

- Research the elements involved. What do you think the message was?

- Going forward, write down any future experiences you have; include details of what you see and feel. Is there any connection to something going on in your life?

What I love about spirit encounters is they let you know the people coming through are OK. They are with you and supporting you. If you have the opportunity and ability to communicate, honor and respect that gift, but do not forget to set boundaries not only for them but for yourself. Also be sure to take time to build and restore your energy.

Guides

Guides are with you throughout your life, guiding you when you are not even aware; they are the messengers of your soul. Sometimes, it is comforting to call on your Guides for extra support, calmness, and strength. I love knowing they are always there.

The number of Guides you have is unique to you. While I have several, only a couple of mine have appeared to me so far. If you have not received visits from your own Guides, do not worry. They are still there and available to you at any time.

My Guide visits occur at night and are a similar experience to that of spirits: my eyes pop open and there they are.

While some come through as dark, translucent orbs and discs, most encounters share the following features.

- I can see them in full color.
- I can see they are from different times and places.
- I can see their clothing and accessories (headwear, jewelry, etc.).
- I can sometimes see a background or environment.

Ethereal Presence

In my first experience, a Guide appeared at the foot of my bed. She was ethereal and medieval in appearance. She wore a white flowing gown in the style of the early Dark Ages. She wore a unique headpiece that had white veils trailing down from two white cones. I did not see specific facial features, but she was slender, stood tall and confident, and felt mature but not old.

Interested to know more about her and her place in history, I did some online research on the Dark Ages. First, I searched images of women's clothing from that period. As I scrolled through the images, I was struck by one in particular—a woman wearing the same style of gown and headpiece as the woman I saw. The only difference was the outfit was not white.

As I did more searching, I discovered my Guide was of the time of the legendary (and often controversial) King Arthur and Guinevere. While I only saw her for a few seconds, her image and energy were memorable. If I had known at the time who she was, I would have attempted to communicate with her and receive her message. Instead, I just closed my eyes to go back to sleep. A missed opportunity.

Double Dose

My next Guide visit was also during the night—and a twofold experience. I first opened my eyes to a black spirit shape by the head of my bed. It had an adult male energy and almost seemed like he was willing me to engage. As I often did, I ignored him and tried to go back to sleep.

Well, he was not giving up that easily. Within moments, my eyes popped open again. This time, I was visited by a man in his late thirties or early forties and in full color. I felt he was of average height, with dark hair shaved close to his head and closely shaved facial hair. He wore a plaid shirt and jeans. He actually felt to be a fairly modern man, like someone I could have seen anywhere. Once again, I ignored my visitor to try to go back to sleep. What I didn't realize was that it was the same Guide (presented in a more recognizable form); he was just more persistent in trying to get my attention.

You might think I would jump at the opportunity to talk to these visitors. However, at the time, I did not know they were my Guides coming to me with messages for my journey. I assumed they were just more spirits interrupting my sleep. I suppose I should have known they were different, if for no other reason than they appeared in full color.

It was not until I talked to my mentor that she told me they were my Guides and had messages for me. My response? "Guess I should have talked to them instead of shushing them away." Of course, that is exactly what I should have done! Lesson learned.

Here is the thing: not everyone is given the gift of being able to connect to and communicate with their Guides or even any spirits. Knowing of this ability, I will certainly be sure to communicate with any who visit me going forward, especially when they appear in full color!

Spirits and Guides are an amazing facet of spirituality, and the messages they are trying to give you relate directly to your *Life Cleansing* journey. When your Guides come through from other places and times, they are encouraging you to research and interpret what you see—whether richness or poverty, politics or religion, peace or war. Study the qualities represented by their time and environment; consider what their life was like and how it could have been different. Most importantly, recognize how the encounter made you feel.

MAKING ROOM FOR YOUR INNER CHILD

Your inner child can be a wonderful participant in your self-discovery—it is there to support you and remind you to stop and have some fun along the way. Your inner child can help you tap into your imagination and creativity, inspire enthusiasm, remind you not to take life too seriously, and urge you to seek opportunities to play and laugh (sometimes even at yourself).

It is not unusual that the older you become, the more consumed with work and responsibilities you get and the further you stray from your inner child. Have you lost your inner child? Staying connected takes intentional work, and it is important work.

If you have trouble remembering or connecting with happy childhood memories, that is OK. There are plenty of other ways to tap into your inner child.

⟫⟫⟫ **DISCOVERY EXERCISE** ⟪⟪⟪

Consider the following list of things you can do to tap into your inner child. Start by opening your birth code and stating you are open to connecting with your inner child. Choose to do an activity from the following list (or your own).

- Buy something that triggers your inner child. Choose whatever you are energetically drawn to—something that, when you look at it, will remind you to lighten up and take some time to have fun.

- Place a favorite childhood picture on display, one that makes you smile when you look at it.

- Buy a toy or game that is the same or similar to something you loved as a child.

- Think back to what you did for fun as a child, and do some of those things now.

- Find video clips online of small children being silly, playing, and laughing. Chances are you will start smiling and maybe even giggling too; sometimes, just hearing a child's laughter is all it takes.

- Pick a fun game and invite friends over for game night.

- Turn on your favorite music. Sing like nobody can hear you, and dance like nobody can see you.

- Go to a children's animated movie.

- Attend a children's theater production.

- Sign up for an acting or improv class.

How did doing that activity make you feel?

Sometimes, watching a child can take you back to a childhood memory you completely forgot about. I sometimes may end up feeling negative emotions. First, I get all wrapped up in the happy feelings, the playfulness, the lack of restraint in the child's play, laughter, and excitement. But there are times when the happy feelings are followed by sad feelings, as though I am grieving the loss of my own childlike spirit. I feel sad that I cannot remember when I last felt like that fun, spunky little girl who loved to play with baby pigs and make mud pies. Perhaps I feel this more intensely because I never had children and did not have that energy around to remind me. When you feel this way, it is the perfect time to allow yourself to be completely silly! Do not even think about it; just do something completely childlike and carefree.

⋙ DISCOVERY EXERCISE ⋘

Make mud pies! As a child, I made these with actual mud. Recently, I made them using various food items and shaped them into smiley faces.

1. Over the course of a week or two, pick a time and get started. Play some fun music in the background.

2. Get a plate or something flat to put your creation onto. (Note: This is *not* the type of pie you bake and eat!)

3. Go through your refrigerator and food cabinets, pulling out any items you could use in your mud pies. Be creative. However, if you want to be authentic, get outside, make some mud, and scrounge for things in the environment to add character to your pie.

4. When you have finished making your pie, make note of how you felt throughout the process. If you are like me, you will be giggling the whole time.

5. Take a picture of your mud pie. Keep the photo handy for when you just need a smile and a reminder of how you felt.

In my *Life Cleansing* work, one piece of homework involved writing down all the ways I could be impish (i.e., mischievous, rascally). In other words, what things would I like to do that others would not expect of me? It was a difficult exercise, as I had always been reserved, shy, and in control of my behavior.

When I finally created my list, there was a freedom and friskiness to the "impish" items . . . but sadness, as well, in realizing I had not done any of these things for many years, if ever. I was all work and no play. I let my career and stress suffocate me without even realizing it.

Now that I have rediscovered my inner child, I keep her close.

⫸ DISCOVERY EXERCISE ⫷

Write down all the ways you could be impish and answer the following questions. (Just to be clear—this does not include illegal activities.)

- How did this exercise make you feel before you started your list?

- How did this exercise make you feel after your list was completed?

You have your list—now choose three of your ideas and do them!

It is important to be true to yourself and honest about what fun means and looks like to *you*. What others consider fun may not be fun for you, so be careful not to allow them to control it for you. Otherwise, they will get frustrated when you do not share or express their same enthusiasm; what should be fun becomes stressful and unsatisfying.

You need to be honest and communicative—share your own ideas of fun with others. Perhaps you need to do things on your own, or even find some new or additional friends who enjoy what you do. Fun does not have to be all or nothing.

Sometimes, opportunities to connect with your inner child appear in unexpected ways.

Little Boy on a Plane

When I travel by plane, I always wonder who will be seated next to me. While on a short trip by myself, I had the pleasure of sitting next to an adorable six-year-old boy. He was well-mannered and sweet, yet he was also a typical little boy . . . making farting noises with his hands and cheeks, jumping in his seat, and begging to play games.

I got the sense he was a boy seeking loving attention (his dad was intoxicated and more concerned with drinking his wine than entertaining his son). So, I became the little boy's new friend. Even though I was not in a playful mood, I went ahead and played a coloring game with him on his electronic device, along with a card game. As a reward, he gave me the sticker he had received from the security agent at the airport.

When we exited the plane, he skipped along behind me and said he was going to follow me wherever I go! How could I not get the message that was being sent? My inner child is always with me; I just need to pay attention.

Laughing Ladies

Laughter is always a good thing and an instant mood lifter. While on a trip overseas, my group had stopped at a tourist destination. As I was walking around by myself, I came upon two older women from England, giggling like little girls while looking at something on their phones. I just had to approach them and find out what they were giggling about.

Apparently, they were trying to take a photo of themselves on their phone camera, but it just was not working out well. Of course, I offered to take the photo for them, and I had trouble too! To our dismay, we finally figured out that the setting was on video. We were all rolling with laughter as we realized it had recorded all the silly things we were saying during our photo-taking attempts. It was a hilarious, unexpected moment of pure joy!

Life moves so fast. It can be intense and stressful, which means it is more important than ever to remember your inner child and have some fun!

HOW PAST LIVES CAN HELP
YOU IN THE PRESENT

There are things going on in your current life that you are repeating from a past life, and they represent behaviors or patterns connected to your core issue in this life.

Once you understand your core issue, then you can do homework to release those patterns and behaviors from your life, which will ultimately help you understand your higher purpose. That is the backbone of *Life Cleansing*.

Sometimes it takes digging into multiple lives to get all the messages and guidance you need. Do not worry or feel you are lacking if you are not able to connect to past lives. Not everyone is given the ability, and that is OK—as you are learning in this book, there are many elements to spiritual self-discovery, and this is just one of them. As with all the elements in this book, what you open to will be unique to you and your journey.

Past life experiences are not easy to access, and, in some rare instances, they can be on the dark side. They are also not easy to connect to, as, in some instances, you may be resisting what that life is trying to tell you. Past lives are revealed to you for a reason: to help you resolve your core issue.

So, how do you know if you have entered a past life? While experiences are unique to the individual, here are ways I have experienced past life exposure:

- Whether it is through a dream or meditation, what I see just *feels* different. Instead of being *in* the dream and seeing all the layers and symbols it is trying to show me, I feel like I am floating above a scene and watching it being replayed like a memory. While I am not in it as I appear in my current life, I *know* it is me that I am seeing. The sight feels *real* and *surreal* at the same time.

- I feel myself taking in all the details of every person in the scene—their gender, clothing, age, facial features, hair color, body shape, social status, and possible occupation.

- I notice every detail of the location and environment—if it is in a home, place of work, some other building, or an outside environment. I also notice the time of year and weather.

- I get a sense of what I and others are feeling in that scene—sadness, anger, anticipation, joy, confusion, grief, fear, and so on.

● I get a sense of time—the approximate century and whether the year is AD or BC. If a past life is revealed as a date, I can usually tell if it is AD or BC by the way I feel or the manner the date or scene is revealed.

When an actual date is revealed, I research events during that time in history. As I look through the events, I pay attention to where I feel energy hits (intuition), as these tell me what I need to know. Then I research that event further (people, places, culture, clothing, society, industry, conflicts, politics, religion, education, etc.). Again, my energy will give hits when I am closing in on the past life it wants me to access.

All the past lives I have accessed have been very unique and from all spans of time. Some involved the Taj Mahal; sixteenth-century France, Wales, and England; late nineteenth-century rural America; ancient Greece; the Great Famine of Europe; and early twentieth-century America. These are just some of the lives I have been able to access. There have also been other interesting times in history included on my journey—they each served a purpose.

A few of the above past lives have been instrumental to my journey, and I have discovered many interesting twists and turns. One unexpected aspect about accessing past lives is discovering connections to your current ancestry. This ties in with the energy you may feel when visiting certain places (or when on a vision quest, discussed later).

To give you an idea of how past lives can assist with *Life Cleansing,* following is a brief summary of messages from my experiences:

- There were habits and patterns in that life that I was re-creating in this life. There was also residual energy from that life influencing decisions in my current life. Through gaining an understanding of what life was like in those times as a member of the royal court, I was able to see correlations to current struggles in my life and determine what actions I needed to take to honor my self-integrity and spiritual power. This was the life most connected to my core issue—almost all the homework on my journey tied back to this life.

- I need to be proud of what I create and not worry if someone does not like my work. I need to stay true to myself and create what I feel I need to create. I need to engage my heart, not my ego.

- I cannot be afraid to take risks and put myself out there and among people; I need to say yes to opportunities to live a wonderful life.

- I am validated in my current life as a strong and confident woman free to live the life I wish.

- Amid despair, there is hope and there are things that are good; it is not all drudgery and gloom.

- Sometimes what we want is not what we need. It is important that I write this book and future books. What I am writing is not just for the present; it is for a lifetime and future generations. People need what I have to share. It needs to be timeless.

When you think of your soul as being limited to your current life, you reject valuable insights and information. Your soul has possibly lived thousands of lives, and each is there to help you learn and be your best self for whatever amount of time you are here.

DREAMS: MAKING SENSE OUT
OF WHAT DOES NOT

As I mentioned earlier, *wishes* state *what* you want. *Dreams* show you
how. Dreams provide you with layers of symbolism and messages
that either validate your direction or provide you with needed guidance. Through interpreting the many layers of your dreams, you
receive amazing insight into where your soul and your Guides are
leading you. It is important that you focus on your current dreams,
not those you have had in the past. Your dreams are a reflection of
what you are working on (or need to work on) in the present.

Not everyone dreams the same way or amount as others.
It depends on where you are on your own spiritual journey,
whether you have a young soul or a very old soul, and how
open you are to receive.

Many books and online resources provide interpretations of the symbolism of dreams. My purpose is not to give

you more interpretations but rather to help you understand many of the elements involved in dreams based on my own experience and learning.

What Is in a Dream?

As you will see in the following sections, dreams can be packed with information.

ENVIRONMENT

- Were you in a house (familiar or unfamiliar)?
- Were you in a structure (occupied or abandoned)?
- What did the structure look like?
- What was the structure made of (wood, concrete)?
- What was the age of the structure (new or old)?
- Did you see every detail of the interior space, or was it just an external facade?
- Were you in your home country or a foreign country?
- Were you in a city or a rural area?
- Were you in an outside space?

FEELINGS

- What were the feelings being expressed in the dream?
- What were you feeling inside the dream?
- How did you feel about the dream when you recalled it?

ELEMENTS AND NATURE

- Was there water (river, stream, lake, pond, ocean; flood, rain, snow, ice)?

- What was the land like (forested, barren, mountainous, flat, hilly)?

- What was the sky like (sunny, partially sunny, cloudy; thunderstorms, tornadoes, lightning, rainbows)?

- Was there fire (large fire, bonfire, outdoor grilling)?

- What was the time of day (morning, day, night, dawn, dusk)?

- What was the season (spring, summer, autumn, winter)?

ANIMALS

- What was it?

- Was there more than one type?

- How many were there?

- What color was it?

- How was it behaving (playful, frightened, protective; fighting, charging, eating, foraging)?

- Was it contained, or was it free?

- Where was it? Was it in its natural habitat?

SYMBOLS

Aside from the categories listed in this section, symbols also appear as colors, shapes, numbers, and other miscellaneous objects (refer to "Getting Clarity Through Signs and Symbols").

PEOPLE

When there are people in your dream, that person is representing some part of you (you are everyone in the dream). As such, it is important to understand what each person (there is seldom just one) represents.

- Who were they (you, family members, friends, people you dislike, colleagues, ex-spouses or partners, relatives, strangers)?

- What were they doing (searching, running, walking, hiding, escaping, climbing, falling, riding, driving, following, playing, eating, drinking, dancing, singing)?

- How were they feeling (happy, frightened, embarrassed, determined, confused, angry, rejected, accepted)?

- What role did/do they play in your life?

- What qualities and/or behaviors was the person exhibiting (controlling, supporting, observing)?

- What did/do you like about those people?

- What irritated you about those people?

It fascinates me to dream of people I do not know and places I have never been. In one particular dream, I was in a place in Germany; while researching a past life, I came across that exact place. (Coincidence? I do not think so.) Dreams can be *very* bizarre. But when you interpret all the layers, they will give you important messages that make sense for what you are working on in your life.

Sometimes dreams are dark and heavy; these are what I would categorize as *nightmares.* You may wake up with a racing heart, your whole body sweating, and wonder why you would dream something so dark and frightening. These types of dreams come from your shadow side—an extreme side of who you are that your conscious self does not see or want to see, often representing your fears, desires, and worries.

These dark nightmares reveal your fears or show you how it could be to have something taken to the negative extreme. They demonstrate that you can push yourself beyond your current or perceived boundaries and control but not actually take it to the negative extreme. Please do not worry if you have this type of dream. Again, as with other dreams, it is a way to give you a message about yourself (which is positive) and connect to your core issue from another perspective. Good or bad, it is all about your journey.

Every once in a great while, I will have a sad dream, often involving a loved one or sometimes a former significant other. It may be a situation where there is illness, death, or a feeling of loss, and I am crying. This type of dream shows you have the ability to connect with that person's energy. You are sensing that the person is at a point or in the process of making a critical choice about his or her life. Following a dream like this, you may feel the need to reach out to that person if they are someone you still have access to.

I will admit, I do not like these types of dream connections. They can be very emotionally draining and make you feel heavy. Thankfully, they are a rare occurrence. If you experience one, take time to process the feelings and energy, take action if you feel the need to do so, and then release it.

Sometimes dreams are so real and interactive that you feel like you are participating in the dream. In one dream, I was at an unfamiliar home in a residential area and saw myself walking up the steps, opening the door, and walking through every room. I saw every detail and felt the emotions of the space. This has happened in other structures as well. Dreams like this often show you a space representing a feeling from a place in your past. They are letting you know you can move on; it no longer has a hold on you.

Some people have recurring dreams. I had a dream like this when I was around age seven and had it numerous times over several years. It was about a girl who was abducted by a man and ultimately murdered. As it was many years ago, I no longer recall any of the details. I just know this dream always frightened me because it felt so real. It was years later when I was an adult and a case like this was all over the news in my state. I remember getting an odd feeling when I heard about it—I immediately thought of that recurring dream I had as a child. I had another dream a few years ago that was also very vivid; it felt current and relevant to our world's current political environment, but it has not happened in real life. Perhaps these dreams were a form of foretelling, or perhaps they were just providing messages for my life at that time.

⫸ DISCOVERY EXERCISE ⫷

What are you dreaming? Over the course of two weeks, record every dream you have.

- Write down all the details of your dream. (Refer to the sections noted earlier in the chapter.)

- Research the elements of your dream.

- Based on the information you discover, what is the message being relayed to you? Is the dream providing you with validation, or is it guiding you to behaviors you need to bring into your life?

It is helpful to review all your dream interpretations over the time period, as you may notice a pattern forming. Pay attention.

Dreams can be powerful. That is why it is so important to really dissect and understand every element of each dream. I have documented and interpreted hundreds of my dreams. Every single one has been different, and every single one has had a useful message. Do not be afraid of dreams; they come through to help you. If you are having dreams, it means you are open to receiving the messages they provide, and that is a gift.

Always keep a pen and notepad by your bed and write down *everything* that comes to you while you sleep! Ask yourself…Was it a visit? Was it a past life? Was it a prediction? Was it really *just* a dream?

VISION QUEST: FEELING THE PAST, LIVING THE PRESENT

Do you ever find yourself pondering your place in the world? You may wonder where you belong or where your true home is. Do you believe you are meant to be somewhere other than where you are?

When I thought about this myself, the answer I came to is *the world is where I belong*. I am not meant to be in just one place, living the same day over and over. I want to live a curious and adventurous life.

While the United States of America is where my ancestors settled, where I was born, where I live, where I receive mail, and where I pay taxes, I consider myself a citizen of the Universe. When you are living your higher purpose as your true self, your home is wherever you are—because where you are is where you are meant to be.

Have you ever felt a strong pull toward a certain place where something inside you feels connected? If yes, find a way to spend some time there. Allow yourself that feeling of rightness and fulfillment. This yearning is about the promise and possibility of all the people you are meant to meet and experiences you are meant to have. It is also likely you are feeling the pull of past lives. Maybe it is time for a vision quest.

A vision quest, in my interpretation and experience, is about connecting with the energies of past lives, feeling a connection to the environment, working on your core issue, and self-validation. Vision quests are individually unique and can be carried out in many ways—they have been a part of many cultures for many centuries.

How did I know when to take my vision quest?

- I had spent a couple of years working hard on my core issue and had reached a point where I felt solid in my true self.

- I had discovered additional genealogical information on my family.

- I had researched some of my past lives connected to a specific area of Europe. (For years, I had felt a strong pull toward this exact area.)

- I had received numerous signs and symbols related to the area I was drawn toward.

- I just knew, energetically, that it was time.

It also became apparent to me that my vision quest was to involve extensive world travel. Vision quests involve many different experiences; yours will be unique to you.

Once I was ready, I started considering travel dates and specific countries I wanted to explore. My original plan was to take a two-week trip to Ireland and Scotland. I researched various tour companies, chose one I had used in the past, selected the trip that covered the most area in a two-week period of time, reviewed the itinerary, selected the dates, and scoped out potential flights. Then, something interesting happened.

Just when I was about to move ahead to book the trip, I felt the need to scroll through all the tour options one more time. As I did so, I felt a strong energy hit on a different trip from the one I had planned. My vison quest had now become a four-week trip to England, Wales, Ireland, Northern Ireland, and Scotland. I was filled with excitement and energy!

It was then time to do some homework in preparation for my vision quest. This involved going through the entire itinerary and choosing (energetically) several places from each country I felt drawn to and reflecting on why I was drawn to them. I researched a few of them in more depth and again recorded my feelings. This interesting part of the process helped me feel where my connections were.

At the same time, I continued doing homework related to further understanding my true self, preparing me to be fully engaged in my vision quest. Prior to leaving on my trip, I prepared specific homework for the trip itself—a way to keep me engaged, push me out of my comfort zone, and break some of my habits and patterns. I was ready to go!

Before I knew it, I was embarking on my journey. I joined a tour group with forty-two other people along with a tour guide and tour driver. I knew I was going to be in full-time processing mode—that is a lot of personalities—but I looked forward to meeting everyone and experiencing every moment of the trip.

As you can imagine, there were hundreds of incredible moments, and the scenery was beyond compare. Best of all, I was able to simply be me; nobody knew me, my background, my family, my relatives, or my work. I felt liberated and restriction-free!

I was intentional about my choices during the trip. I processed my feelings about myself, the other passengers, other people, the places, the culture, and the scenery, and I expressed my thoughts and opinions. I allowed myself to feel passion for all my experiences but particularly for a special few, and I paid great attention to my energy and that of others, as well as that of the places and of the scenery.

It was intense. *Throughout all the countries, the energy I felt in some places was incredibly strong; I just knew I had been there before. Some environments felt very peaceful and reflective, some felt raw and electrified, and some had stillness in one spot but strong movement in another.*

What caught me by surprise was the all-consuming emotion I felt when passing through many areas of Scotland, especially the Highlands. As I looked at the scenery pass by, I started crying. In another area of the Highlands, as I looked out the window, I had a vision from centuries past. The energy and emotion felt so real and, again, I started crying. That is what was so amazing about my vision quest—it was unique, it was unexpected, and it was encompassed by energy and emotion. There was an incredible rightness to the whole experience.

When we were all dropped off at our final hotel before departing to our home cities, I was overwhelmingly emotional. While I had felt this to some degree on all my international trips, it was clear this was like no other trip. I knew I was about to break down, so I quickly said some special goodbyes, went to my hotel room, and cried on and off for several hours. I did not want to go home; I belonged there. I belonged in Scotland.

If you love to travel, exploring other places and meeting people of other countries and cultures, landing back in your reality can be really difficult. Upon returning home, you may experience what I call *post-trip depression*. It is that consuming feeling that you just want to be back over there. It feels almost impossible to reengage in your normal life. As my vision quest was so intertwined with my core issue, following are a couple of pieces of homework that helped me land back in my homelife:

- I had to write about how I was over there—what qualities of my true self were present, how those qualities showed up, how I felt about being my true self—and then write down how I could be that way here at home.

- I had to write about how my experiences felt over there—which experiences stood out and why, how those experiences reflected my true self, how they represented my core issue, where I broke habits and patterns—and then write down how I could bring those into being here at home.

Sometimes what you are looking for is right in front of you, where you are. You do not always have to go on a vision quest or be in another country to be the person you are and have the experiences you want.

So, if you find yourself yearning to be back *over there*, or anywhere else that pulls at your soul, continue to work at finding out what you need and being who you need to be, wherever you are. It is up to you to define the life you want and then do the work. Perhaps your vision quest will reveal new ways to approach your *Life Cleansing* work—ways to clear your physical and emotional space to make room for all the new possibilities. Maybe you will even come up with some new wishes!

VIBES: WHAT YOU DO NOT SEE

Have you ever met a person you immediately felt connected to and comfortable with? Perhaps when you met this person, it felt like you had known them forever. Every interaction has a different vibe, and reading that vibe is like being a detective deciphering a mystery.

Feeling vibes is, in my opinion, really fun. Pay attention to how people, places, and environments make you feel. Everything has energy.

PEOPLE

- Do they feel genuine or fake?
- Do you trust them? Why or why not?
- Do you feel threatened by them?
- Do you feel welcomed by them?
- Do they bring energy and life to the room or drag it down?

PLACES

- Does the place feel sad?

- Does it feel happy?

- Do you feel like you are welcome?

- Do you feel like you are in danger?

- Do you feel like you are being watched?

- Do you feel like it is holding secrets?

There may be times when you interact with someone and feel a strange or negative vibe. If so, you need to ask yourself a few questions.

- Do you feel it is related to your current life?

- Do you feel it is related to a past life?

- Is the reaction truly about the other person, or is it about you?

- Is any further interaction needed with that person or situation? If no, then move on; do not allow the negativity to waste your energy.

When an Intuitive Meets a Medium

How strange was it to get a tense vibe from a fellow intuitive and medium? I had never been read by a medium before, and I had always been fascinated by their abilities. This particular medium was at a private event to talk about intuition and affirmations as well as to do a few readings for attendees.

I was out in the lobby, talking to a couple of women, when I saw the medium walk by. We made brief eye contact. Immediately, I felt a vibe, and I wondered if she felt a vibe about me as well.

In the session, after speaking a little while, she asked us to raise our hands if we would like to be read. I obviously raised my hand as did many others. As she talked and quickly scanned the room, I just knew I would be first. She turned, looked right at me, and (you guessed it) said she was going to read me first.

First, she put her hand on her stomach (area of the third chakra) and made statements about me and how I hold my energy. It was all true. Next, she mentioned someone being a teacher . . . which probably sounded strange to an audience of administrative professionals. However, it was not strange to me. Why? Earlier that evening, while she was talking to us, I wrote in my notebook "I am a Teacher" *in large letters. She went on to tell a personal story about a teacher, and I understood everything conveyed.*

She then went on to do readings for a few other attendees. They were connections to people who had crossed over; I was the only one to get personal messages directly. Even though she read me, I continued to feel that strange vibe with her throughout the rest of the evening as well as after the session, when I asked her a question. There was just something off, and we both felt it. It was clear she was not comfortable with me either, based on her body language.

So, why such strange vibes? It turned out the medium and I had been at odds in a past life. However, by both of us engaging—the medium reading me and me being open to hearing her message—the interaction provided closure to that past life conflict.

Observation and Sight

What is the difference between observation and sight? *Observation* is external and allows you to see what is all around you—people, body language, places, activities, and objects. *Sight* is internal and allows you to see into others, to feel their energy, and to understand nuances about them, some of which they may not even know themselves.

While both observation and sight require you to pay attention to everything else outside of you, you do need to pay attention to your internal energy. Utilizing these skills involves being open and not making assumptions or judgments. You will feel yourself become more aware and able to process what you observe or see more quickly and accurately. You not only need to process how you feel about what you are observing or seeing, you also need to process your thoughts and reactions to what you are observing or seeing.

Developing and using these skills can be a great asset in your work. It is a very strong area for me; I see much deeper into people and situations than they realize. This was especially true in professional meetings or at large events, where I would make observations and provide insights to my boss or other appropriate people involved. These were really valuable to them, as they did not always catch subtleties that were critical in some situations. It was also interesting to observe people when the boss was in the room and when he was not. Nobody knew how much I really saw and processed. I am great at seeing and listening while appearing not to be—a perk of being an introvert.

These skills can also be helpful when mentoring, coaching, or teaching. They allow you to have a much broader perspective on situations to manage conversations differently or support people in ways they do not realize they need. These skills may also prepare you to ask the questions necessary to get at something deeper, yet in a way in which a person does not feel threatened. This provides for more fluid and natural conversation.

While interacting with someone, do not forget to look into their eyes; it is amazing what you can see and feel, either by a quick glance or a long stare. My grandma swore by this. She had great sight. Some have told me that my eyes are very deep and draw them in, and that my focus gives them a calm feeling, encouraging them to be more open and willing to share what is on their mind. However, there have been times when men felt very uncomfortable when I looked into their eyes longer than they wanted. Perhaps they knew I was seeing more than they wanted me to and it made them nervous! When you are meeting and talking with people, pay attention: do they allow eye contact, or do they look away?

Intuition

How many times have you been told to "go with your gut"? Intuition is your internal energy working through you to help you make the right decisions. Your gut either feels right or it feels wrong. Pay attention!

Following is a personal story about intuition—the difference between just feeling fearful and feeling fearful out of possible danger.

The Trail of Intuition

It was one of those idyllic spring days one rarely gets the opportunity to enjoy, but I had that opportunity.

I had gone to a local park, one of my favorites, and decided it would be a great afternoon to walk the trail running adjacent to the river through our small town. I had walked this trail a couple of other times and was always cautioned by others to be careful. That day, I decided I would bring my pepper spray but keep it tucked away. I was sure I would not need to use it.

The trail entrance was just a short walk from my apartment. As soon as I stepped onto the trail, I got an uneasy feeling. Then I noticed a man just ahead of me. He was talking on his phone as he walked along and veered up a hill. I continued on my walk. My goal was to cut in on at least three of the narrow dirt paths along the paved trail. Even with the uneasiness I was feeling, I continued on and walked down the first dirt path. As I went in, I noticed it branched off to other paths; upon hearing some male voices, I decided to turn back to the main trail.

Some distance in front of me, I noticed a man had just gotten up from a bench about a third of the way down the main trail. I immediately felt my hackles raise. I watched the guy, still at some distance, walk very slowly toward me. As he got a little closer, I touched my waist area (signaling like I was maybe carrying a form of protection). My phone was in my left hand.

As he got closer, I noticed his appearance. I was not really afraid of him; he looked harmless enough. Yet I felt the strong need to memorize every possible detail. As he passed by me, I continued to look right at him and said hello. He hesitated for a moment but then responded hello as well and continued walking at his slow pace.

My hackles were still raised, so I waited a minute or two before looking back; he was still walking. At this time, I saw a couple farther back on the trail, looking up to the side, perhaps bird-watching. (Note: I never did see that couple after that, anywhere on the trail.)

I continued walking and, with leeriness, went down two more side dirt paths. Because I was still feeling uneasy, I continued to look behind me and, with a little more speed, finished my walk out to the street at the end of that trail.

Then it was time to walk back. Now carrying my pepper spray, I walked on. I noticed the man I had seen earlier walking back toward me. As he got closer, I noticed he was now carrying his sweatshirt, sweating heavily, and walking strangely. This time, he looked down more as he passed by, but I looked right at him again. Then I was back to the main street and on my way home.

A few days later, I found out the guy was the likely suspect of some trail robberies. After another park incident that same week,

I called the police and gave a full report of both incidents. The police told me the suspect had not been caught yet and there had actually been an incident the very day and time of my trail walk. My uneasiness being on the trail that day was based on possible danger, and my energy had alerted me to it.

I had to wonder why I was not his target that day. Perhaps it was because I walked tall and confidently, looked fit, and had things in my hands. Maybe it was because I did not look or act afraid; I looked him in the eye, engaged in talk, and watched him intently.

While the outcome of my walk could have been different, it made me clearly aware of the power of my intuition. It was a great lesson in learning the difference between fear (not wanting to do or try something) and intuition (possibility of danger). As I love to travel and explore on my own, this was an invaluable experience.

The moral of the story? Walk tall with confidence and awareness, pay attention, and trust your intuition!

Residual Energy

Have you ever walked into a space and immediately felt like someone was there with you?

What you are feeling is residual energy from the past. This is not necessarily a spirit but rather an imprint of energy from a person or event in that space. Residual energy does not only exist in houses or buildings but also in outdoor spaces and ruins.

Similar to spirits, you may feel other characteristics of residual energy of a space, such as sadness, anger, fear, or happiness. It may even feel like it is welcoming you.

If you experience this feeling once, you will likely be open to feeling it at other times as well. Perhaps this is one reason you may find it difficult to sleep peacefully in hotels or other peoples' homes; your energy is always feeling and connecting.

Not Alone in the Basement

I have never liked the basement in my oldest sister's home, but I also never had much reason to be down there, even though it is completely finished and part of their overall living space. One night, I had to sleep on the basement couch because the spare bedrooms upstairs were being used. As I got blankets and a pillow to settle in for the night, I felt uneasy. I felt like I was not alone, that there was some kind of energy down there. When I mentioned this to my sister a couple of weeks later, she said it was no wonder: a former resident had died in the basement of that home.

Walk Around Town

Autumn is my favorite time of year, with the cool air and beautiful colors of the trees. On a couple of perfect afternoons, I decided to go for a walk around town and photograph unique historic homes and buildings. It was interesting how different each structure felt— strong, stoic, prominent, warm, cold. Some felt fun and whimsical, while others felt foreboding and secretive. When looking at my photos, I also discovered orbs of different shapes and colors.

History Overseas

While on my vision quest, I had the opportunity to stay in a number of hotels and visit many historical places. Every place had its own feel: the quiet solitude and heaviness in the crypt at Canterbury Cathedral, the strong winds at Stonehenge, the peace of Glastonbury Abbey, and the stillness and mystery of Clava Cairns.

Then there was a hotel room in England—as soon as I walked into my small room, I could feel energy there with me. Between the residual energy and a couple of issues with the room, sleep was not to be had that evening. The next morning, while talking to a couple of other guests and comparing features of our rooms, we wondered if the hotel had once been something else. With that thought in mind, I went to the front desk and inquired about the history of the hotel. No wonder I felt such uneasy energy in my room; it had once been a general hospital as well as a war hospital.

Another form of energy you may feel is the environment around you. Walk into a restaurant or bar and you can tell if the energy is positive or negative just by the people occupying the space. As some leave and others enter, the energy changes.

Sometimes a space just feels stale and sad. Have you ever gone back to a former employer and your former work area no longer feels the same? That is because your energy is no longer there; it is no longer intertwined in that environment. It is similar to standing near a train track as a train goes by; you hear it coming, you feel its power, and then it is gone . . . and there is silence once again. This is a great example of why it is so important to love what you do and be aware of the energy you bring into a space; it leaves a lasting imprint.

Remember that you and your energy impact everything and everyone around you.

⫸ DISCOVERY EXERCISE ⫷

What vibes are you getting? Over the course of two weeks, choose three places (e.g., a coffee shop, restaurant, bar, or historical building) to spend some time in and observe for at least thirty minutes.

- What is the place?

- How did the exterior of the building make you feel?

- How did you feel when you first walked in?

- Were there people in there? How did they make you feel?

- What did it feel like over the time you were in there?

- How did you feel when you left?

- Go back to one of the locations a couple of weeks later. Did you experience the same reactions and feelings? If not, what was different?

Paying attention to energy is a very important part of *Life Cleansing*. It helps you determine your interaction with a person, place, or situation, and it can help you gauge your level of openness to the messages being provided to you.

CONNECTING TO AND
STRENGTHENING YOUR CHAKRAS

What comes from within comes from your energy.

Do you understand your energy? Do you know your chakra centers and energy colors? Connecting to your chakras is a great growing exercise that can help you connect with who you are in the most inner and complex way.

As with many spiritual practices, there is more than one way or method. With chakras, you will most commonly see the seven-chakra model. However, I follow a nine-chakra system, as outlined by the Jwalan Muktikā School for Illumination, and that is what I will be sharing with you in this chapter. The model you choose is up to personal preference. Some may be able to tap into and see their individual chakra colors, but do not worry if you cannot. There are also those who have the ability to see and read your colors for you.

Following are the energy centers of the nine-chakra system and a brief description of the chakras and their energy purposes.

1. Base of the spine, commonly called the *root chakra:* stability and grounding in third dimension.

2. Reproductive area, commonly referred to as the *sacral chakra:* birth, creativity, and tantric energy.

3. Near the navel, commonly referred to as the *solar plexus chakra:* personal and spiritual power.

4. In the heart, commonly referred to as the *heart chakra:* love, compassion, and forgiveness.

5. Thymus, a newly remembered chakra and known as the *Seat of the Soul chakra:* where the Spirit enters the body and manifests as the soul.

6. Throat area, commonly called the *throat chakra:* communication and expression of your ideas and visions.

7. In the pituitary gland between the eyebrows, commonly referred to as *the third eye:* insight and inner wisdom.

8. In the pineal gland deep in the brain, known as the *Seat of Source Memory chakra:* universal connection.

9. Crown of the head, commonly referred to as the *crown chakra:* connection to higher consciousness and multiple dimensions.

This is the chakra process I went through following the guidance of my mentor. Every day for two weeks, I set aside time for this work.

- I found a quiet space without distractions.

- I opened my birth code and did deep breathing to clear my mind.

- I put my right hand on each chakra center, breathed deeply and calmly, closed my eyes, and focused on that energy center, five to fifteen minutes each.

- As my eyes were closed, I paid attention to what color(s) appeared. Sometimes it would start as one color then become another. The colors did not always appear in the same area behind my eyes; some appeared in the lower right, some in the middle, and some in the lower left.

- With each chakra, I noted what I felt or if I had any physiological response (e.g., shakiness or vibration, dizziness, rapid heartbeat, increased body heat, an unbalanced or wobbly feeling despite sitting).

- I repeated this for each chakra center. The only variable, I was told, is that black is not an energy color; it represents blockage of that energy center.

Once you get comfortable with your chakra centers, you will be able to more quickly connect to them. The length of time you spend on your chakras is up to you—it could be as little as ten minutes. However, if you feel worried or stressed about something in your life, spend longer on the relevant chakras.

After my initial two weeks, I talked with my mentor, and we discussed my observations, specifically what I thought my color was for each chakra. I noted that some had the same color most or every time, while others were all over the place. After this first round, a few of my chakras were confirmed and refined. I continued this work for another two weeks on the remaining chakras using the same process described above. Then, over another call with my mentor, I confirmed and refined my remaining chakra colors.

In determining chakra colors, there is typically a base color preceded by a descriptor. To give you an example, here are my chakra energy colors:

1. Root = Amethyst purple

2. Sacral = Fuchsia red

3. Solar Plexus = Peacock green

4. Heart = Sapphire blue

5. Seat of the Soul = Plum pink

6. Throat = Rusty copper

7. Third Eye = Cloudy white

8. Seat of Source Memory = Brass yellow

9. Crown = Terra-cotta orange

Do not worry if you are not able to see your own colors; it is much more important that you are working to connect with the energy centers.

You may notice that your chakra energy colors are sometimes lighter and less vibrant. Here are some ways to help enhance that energy:

- Eat healthy foods that reflect your chakra colors, especially in areas where your colors are weak.

- Wear your colors.

- For women, incorporate your colors into jewelry, bags/purses, scarves, shoes, or other fun accessories. For men, incorporate your colors into your ties, socks, shoes, or watches.

- Look at your environment, seek out your energy colors, and focus on them.

- Watch animated children's movies, as they are often filled with vibrant colors. (They also often have great messages.)

Doing these things can make you feel stronger, more confident, and more grounded in your personal and spiritual power. Connecting with your chakras every day, perhaps with your meditation practice, is a great way to begin your day: grounded in *all* your energy!

CREATING INTENTION WITH MEDITATION

Your mind will answer most questions if you learn to relax and wait for the answer.

—*William S. Burroughs*

Meditation helps to heal, replenish, and strengthen your body, mind, and spirit. What a beautiful gift to just be still with yourself, your thoughts, your energy, your healing, your gratitude, and your wishes. Meditation can provide you with great strength, courage, and guidance. It is a great way to connect with the Universe and your higher purpose; it opens you to your possibilities.

Meditation Makes Room for What You Are Meant to Receive

Have you ever decided you were going to meditate only to discover you could not sit still with an empty mind for even a few seconds?

You are not alone! I have heard this statement from almost every person who has attempted to meditate. Meditation looks and sounds pretty easy; however, if you have ever tried it, you know it is far from easy. It never fails that when you take time to meditate, your brain decides to fire thoughts every second. Then you panic because you cannot clear your mind—one thought generates another and another and another, and the last thing you are able to do is focus on your breathing.

Of course, there are some who master meditation quickly. But for most, it takes practice and patience as well as trying various forms of meditation, and even then, some may still never master it. I was one of those people. I tried again and again. I wondered how on earth people can do this for any length of time and look so uninterrupted, peaceful, and tuned out.

I experimented with different poses, furniture, music, and time of day . . . still, nothing worked. I took a break from meditation for a while and opened myself to other ways of quieting my mind. But I knew meditation needed to be part of my life and part of my journey; I had to find a practice that would work for me.

My Steps to Meditation

One morning, while working out on the treadmill and watching TV, I realized I could not stand the television programming and became irritated. I decided to replace it with music. I put together a playlist of favorite songs and timed them to my workout—this worked out great! However, I did not like staring at the wall. So, I went back to the television. One music channel played relaxing music and featured inspirational quotes. Then it clicked! While working out on the treadmill to my playlist, I could mute the television and read the inspirational quotes.

This turned out to be the perfect solution. I was now not only taking care of my physical body but also practicing a form of meditation by focusing my thoughts and energy around those messages. I had found my happy place.

As a side benefit, I learned to keep a pen and notepad on my treadmill. When great thoughts and ideas came to me, I was always ready! (Some even found their way into this book.)

While the treadmill routine worked well for a while, I knew I still wanted dedicated meditation time. I had to somehow create a practice that allowed me to work with the natural movement of my thoughts. I learned to start with focused, intentional thought and gradually transition to absence of thought while achieving a calming and deeply meditative experience.

Before I share my approach, I want you to understand that meditation is a very individual process. What works for me may not be what works for you, and that is OK.

⇛ DISCOVERY EXERCISE ⇚

Figure out your own meditation environment.

- Find a space that works for you. This may take trying out a few different spots.

- Find a time that works for you. Try different times. The *when* is completely your choice, so do not feel you have to do it at an "expected" time like morning (however, morning meditation does provide a great start to the day).

- Determine how much time works for you. Start with small increments and work up to whatever length of time you need or desire.

- Try different things, like sitting in a chair versus on the floor, especially if you have joint issues.

- Decide if you like soft music playing or not. I created a playlist of soothing songs I listen to when I meditate—it is all about personal preference.

- Be as free from distraction as you possibly can, and, if you have others around you, have them support this time. Even if you live in a noisy area, after you find the right meditation and get comfortable doing it, you will get to the point where you are able to zone that external noise out.

- Lastly, do not worry about whether or not you are "doing it right." It is more important that you are simply *doing it*. This is not about being rigid and perfect; it is about being fluid and open.

Now that you have tested your meditation setup, let us move on to the actual meditation practice: moving through intentional thought to absence of thought.

Daily *Life Cleansing* Meditation

The intent of this meditation is not to memorize and repeat the exact same thing to yourself every time. Instead, use the pattern as a guide to help provide focus. Sometimes you may have things come up in your life that you need to bring into the meditation.

Get yourself comfortable, roll your shoulders back to open up your posture, and focus on breathing in and out. Remember, start small. You do not have to do all these every time. The following prompts are what work for me and are intended to help guide you.

In silence . . .

- breathe in life and know how wonderful it is to have life
- breathe in gratitude and state all you are grateful for
- breathe in and connect to your Guides
- breathe in and connect to your animal totems
- breathe in and ask for healing
- breathe in and state your wishes
- breathe in and open your birth code to open you to your possibilities
- breathe in life and ask the Universe to work through you

- breathe and connect with your chakras (I do a full check-in with each of my chakra energy centers)

- breathe in with no thoughts; your mind should now be clear.

Close by saying, "Thank you."

Open your eyes and regain your balance. The energy can be very strong, and you may feel a little shaky.

This process can take as long as you want; it all depends on the specific thoughts you have with each section of the meditation. For me, it can take as little as fifteen minutes or as long as one hour. The more often you do your meditation, the easier it becomes and the deeper and stiller you become. I do this meditation every morning, as it puts me in a peaceful, replenished, focused, and positive mind-set. It gives me energy and courage and prepares me to be a kinder, more compassionate, and grateful person.

In addition to this core meditation, there are also meditations that can be done to help you in other areas of your life, such as work, grief, health, relationships, and even vacation.

Evening *Life Cleansing*

A helpful ritual is to do a *Life Cleansing* exercise before you go to bed at night and when you wake in the morning. You will need a pen and journal on your bedside table (which you should already have for recording any dreams, symbols, or visits you receive).

⋙ **DISCOVERY EXERCISE** ⋘

Before you get into bed . . .

- write down what you want to cleanse from the day.

- write down how you want to replenish your body, mind, and spirit.

- open your birth code to open yourself to any dreams, symbols, visions, or visits that need to be revealed.

During the night, or as soon as you wake . . .

- write down any dreams, symbols, visions, or visits if there were any. (If not, do not worry; they come through when they need to, not necessarily when you want them to.)

When you wake the next morning . . .

- reread what you wanted to replenish.

- research any dreams, symbols, visions, or visits.

- interpret what the Universe is telling you.

There is something else I do once I am in bed: I thank God for my day. I thank God for all the blessings in my life. I ask God to wrap his arms around me, my family, and friends and any others and keep them healthy and safe. I ask God to continue providing me with the strength, guidance, and courage needed for my journey.

I release all negativity and all that is no longer serving me. Lastly, I open my birth code to open myself to whatever needs to be revealed to me. As with meditation, I close by saying, "Thank you."

Meditation is a wonderful and powerful *Life Cleansing* tool.